JOURNEYING
Together
in Christ
THE JOURNEY CONTINUES

JOURNEYING
Together
in Christ
THE JOURNEY CONTINUES

The Report of the
Polish National Catholic
Roman Catholic Dialogue
1989-2002

EDITED BY
MOST REV. ROBERT M. NEMKOVICH
MOST REV. JAMES C. TIMLIN

Our Sunday Visitor Publishing Division
Our Sunday Visitor, Inc.
Huntington, Indiana 46750

Our Sunday Visitor Publishing Division
Our Sunday Visitor, Inc.
200 Noll Plaza
Huntington, IN 46750

ISBN: 1-59276-038-4 (Inventory No. T89)
LCCN: 2003112295

Cover design by Monica Haneline
Interior design by Sherri L. Hoffman

PRINTED IN THE UNITED STATES OF AMERICA

Contents

Introduction

During the dialogue meetings held in October of 2001 in Scranton, Pennsylvania, and May of 2002 in Nashville, Tennessee, the joint commission of the Polish National Catholic-Roman Catholic Dialogue expressed the need and desire for an update to *Journeying Together in Christ: The Report of the Polish National Catholic-Roman Catholic Dialogue.* It was remarked that this first report was issued in 1990 and that much has happened in our respective churches and within the dialogue in the years between then and now. So, with this in mind, we present to the clergy and laity of our respective churches this overview of the dialogue from 1989 until the present time.

It is our desire in publishing this edition that we make the work and concerns of the dialogue the work and concerns of the people of our churches. It is one thing for bishops and clergy to gather together to discuss our respective churches and where we stand on different theological, religious, and administrative matters; but for this work to bear fruit, it must be lived at the level of our parish communities. It is for this reason that we make this book available, so that our communities may not only see the work of this dialogue, but that they may play a role in it. Through discussion, and most especially through prayer, we desire to involve the people of our church communities in the ongoing dialogue between our two churches.

The first volume of *Journeying Together in Christ* covered many of the issues on which the Polish National Catholic Church and the Roman Catholic Church have virtually the same, if not identical, teaching. These dealt with the topics of the role of the sacraments in the life of the church as well as the individual sacraments themselves: baptism, confirmation, Eucharist, penance, anointing of the sick, matrimony, and holy orders. There was also a section on the Word of God, of which, although it is listed as a sacrament in the Polish National Catholic Church, the teaching of the Roman Catholic Church does not differ significantly from that of the Polish National Catholic Church. Lastly, the dialogue report of the first volume dealt with the subject of the Life to Come.

Because of these agreements on matters of faith, the dialogue has been able to move ahead from the time of the first edition of the dialogue report and seek some level of sacramental sharing between our churches. It was during the time period that this present volume covers that Polish National Catholics were afforded the courtesy of Canon 844.3 in regards to receiving the sacraments of penance, Eucharist, and anointing of the sick from ministers of the Roman Catholic Church. Likewise, in later meetings it was recognized that members of the Roman Catholic Church could receive these same sacraments, under certain conditions, from ministers of the Polish National Catholic Church, under Canon 844.2 and paragraph 123 of the 1993 Ecumenical Directory.

Also found within the first volume of *Journeying Together in Christ* were two different versions of the history of the Polish National Catholic Church. One version was written by Joseph W. Wieczerzak, Ph.D., a historian of the Polish National Catholic Church, and one was written by Monsignor John P. Gallagher, Ph.D., a historian of the Roman Catholic Diocese of Scranton. Rather than make an attempt to rewrite these histories or to synthesize these into one history, we present a history of the interactions of the Roman Catholic Church and the Polish National Catholic Church from 1989 up to the present. It will serve as a background to some of the issues that have been discussed at our dialogue meetings.

Our dialogue over the past twelve years can be broken down into essentially four different topics of discussion, although we were certainly not limited in any way in our talks to only these matters. Much time has been spent on our understanding of church and ecclesial structure. As one looks over the topics discussed at the meetings, one can see such topics as: Collegiality of the Roman Catholic Bishops with the Pope, Collegiality of the Polish National Catholic Bishops with the Old Catholic Union of Utrecht, Primacy in the Church, Jurisdiction, The Papacy and the Council, and Petrine Ministry. In all of these matters, we are struggling with our understanding of how the church is to be organized and how it is to operate within our world. We have also dealt with the issue of what parts of these structures, if any, are necessary to the church as a matter of faith.

Secondly, we have dealt with topics on a pastoral level. As was stated above, the Polish National Catholic Church and the Roman Catholic Church now enjoy a certain level of sacramental sharing. In order for this to occur with as little confusion and distraction as possible to the true worship of our people, we must deal with the issues of how this is to take place. Therefore, guidelines have been issued and information disseminated so that all may know that a level of sharing has been accomplished. Also, as part of our discussions on the pastoral aspects of the dialogue, we can place the difficulties that have been encountered on a pastoral level and find resolution for some of them.

As a third general topic of discussion, the dialogue has examined the issues in dealing with union and unity between churches. In these discussions, we have tried to examine what the goals of dialogue between our churches are, for both the short term and long term. While we as Christians seek to follow the prayer of our Lord as He prayed for unity, we still must ask what this unity will look like and how it will be accomplished. In this regard, we have examined, from the Roman Catholic side, the topics of the relationship between the Vatican and the Eastern Catholic churches and the establishment of an Apostolic Administration in Campos, Brazil; and from the Polish National Catholic side, the definition and meaning of full communion between churches and the concept of unity with autonomy and identity. Certainly, in the future this topic will continue to be discussed as we move forward "Journeying Together in Christ."

Our dialogue has dealt with the ecumenical implications of documents that were issued from the Vatican as the fourth point. In particular, we have dealt with *Ut Unum Sint, Dominus Iesus,* and *A Note on the Expression 'Sister Churches.'* These documents, even though not all are directed to an ecumenical audience, have had an effect on this dialogue, as they have had an effect on several dialogues in which the Roman Catholic Church is involved. Each of these documents has been examined for its hopeful points of interaction as well as causes of pain and disappointment. As we continue on in dialogue, we will continue to examine the writings of our respective churches for increased understanding and commitment to dialogue.

The dialogue at the present time stands at a crossroads, or to use the words of Walter Cardinal Kasper, current president of the Pontifical Council for Promoting Christian Unity, we stand at a crisis point. This is not to say that our dialogue has reached a point of impasse, or that some matter has brought it to a stop, but rather that we have trod the easiest part of the journey together as churches. It is apparent there are still many difficult roads ahead. We must now make the choice to continue to discuss these difficult matters in hopes of bringing understanding and agreement.

This dialogue has made great strides in agreement concerning matters of faith and morals. As the first volume of *Journeying Together in Christ* shows, the Polish National Catholic Church and the Roman Catholic Church share the same essential faith in the person and role of our Lord and Savior Jesus Christ within the church; in the holy sacraments as avenues to the receiving of God's grace; and in the ultimate goal of our life, which is union with God in eternity. Along with this basic unity in faith comes a unity in moral outlook toward our society. In this regard, our churches need to strengthen our resolve to continue to spread the Good News of Jesus Christ as the way to salvation and in building the Kingdom of God upon the earth.

As we rejoice in what is held in common, much still needs to be discussed and understood, as our dialogue presses forward. There is still the matter of how the role of the laity is lived within our respective churches, the role of the successor of St. Peter within the church, and how the church is structured. There are still many long and difficult roads ahead on our journey.

This publication, *Journeying Together in Christ: The Journey Continues*, was approved by the members of the Polish National Catholic-Roman Catholic dialogue meeting in Scranton, Pennsylvania, on October 24, 2002. We would like to thank Rev. Robert M. Nemkovich, Jr., and Rev. Anthony A. Mikovsky of the Polish National Catholic Church, and Mr. James B. Earley, Chancellor of the Roman Catholic Diocese of Scranton, for their help and work in the preparation of this volume. Our gratitude is also extended to the many members of the Polish National

Catholic-Roman Catholic Dialogue Team of both the past and the present, for their continued devotion to the work of unity and agreement within the church. We especially wish to remember Rev. John Hotchkin, a dedicated ecumenist and original member of the dialogue, who was called by our Lord to his final reward. We wish to also thank the many dedicated and sincere members of the Polish National Catholic Church and the Roman Catholic Church who, through their work, prayer, and daily lives, further the cause of unity among the people of God.

MOST REV. ROBERT M. NEMKOVICH
Prime Bishop
Polish National Catholic Church

MOST REV. JAMES C. TIMLIN
Bishop of Scranton

A Report on the Polish National Catholic-Roman Catholic Dialogue (1989-2002)

On Thursday, May 3, 1990, a press conference was held in the auditorium at St. Stanislaus Polish National Catholic Cathedral in Scranton, Pennsylvania, to release *Journeying Together in Christ: The Report of the Polish National Catholic-Roman Catholic Dialogue*. This volume provided the faithful of both churches with a summary of the dialogue that had taken place during the period 1984-1989. Members of the dialogue team had been meeting in the spring and fall of each year since the formal start of the talks on October 23, 1984.

For the first time, members of the clergy and laity of both PNCC and RC congregations were able to learn that there was much common ground shared by the two churches that had been separated since 1897, the year in which Father Francis Hodur established the Polish National Catholic Church. *Journeying Together in Christ* provided ample proof that the initial dialogue sessions had shown that both churches shared similar beliefs about the sacraments, Sacred Scripture, and a common understanding about heaven and hell, as well as the universal call to holiness. With so much in common, those members of the dialogue team who gathered in South Scranton for the press conference were eager to release the summary of the talks. They also wanted to voice their hopes for the future.

Present at the press conference were the co-chairmen of the dialogue, Bishop Anthony M. Rysz of the Central Diocese of the PNCC and Bishop Stanislaus J. Brzana, Bishop of Ogdensburg. They were joined by representatives of both churches. For the PNCC, present were: Bishop Joseph I. Nieminski, Bishop of the Canadian Diocese; Father Senior Sigmund Peplowski; Father A. Waine Kargul; and Father Senior Stanley Skrzypek. The RC representatives at the press conference were: Bishop James C. Timlin, Bishop of Scranton; Bishop Alfred L. Abramowicz, Auxiliary Bishop of Chicago; and Rev. John Hotchkin, director of the Ecumenical and Interreligious Affairs Office of the National Conference of Catholic Bishops (known today as the United States Conference of Catholic Bishops).

Many of the reporters wanted to know if unity between the two churches was at hand. They wanted to know not *if* but rather *when* there would be an announcement that the two churches would reunite. Bishop Brzana said, "We cannot put God under a calendar." He insisted that reunification depended on progress made during the future dialogue sessions and on God's grace. Seeking to emphasize that the churches had embarked on a long journey whose outcome was unknown, Bishop Rysz said: "The fact that we are talking is a miracle in itself. As far as where the talks will lead us . . . the hope of all ecumenical encounter is the union of people and the unity of Christ. But that belongs to God."

Journeying Together in Christ was sought by clergy and laity of both churches who wanted insights into what had been discussed during the ten sessions that had occurred between October 1984 and June 1989, the last session before the release of the volume. The participants in the dialogue felt an obligation to issue a report that would communicate that many misunderstandings had been removed and that real common ground about central issues of the Catholic faith had been discovered. Bishop Nieminski commented on the experience of serving on the dialogue team: "It's been a real pleasure for me and a learning experience to participate in the meetings of this joint commission. This dialogue has forced Polish National Catholics also to study their roots. There are fewer misconceptions now, and I think that has helped us in our journeying together in Christ."

Journeying Together in Christ was disseminated in the Scranton area by both church communities. In addition, Our Sunday Visitor, the publisher of the volume, advertised its availability in areas with high concentrations of Polish American Catholics. The book continued to generate great interest.

The Eighteenth General Synod of the PNCC was convened in Toronto on October 1-5, 1990. Prime Bishop John F. Swantek had extended an invitation to Archbishop Daniel E. Pilarczyk, president of the National Conference of Catholic Bishops, to attend the synod. Because the Archbishop was in Rome at the time on other business, Bishop Brzana was afforded an opportunity to address the delegates at the October 4, 1990 session. He said:

Now as you know, an official ecumenical dialogue has been going on between representatives of the Polish National Catholic Church and our Roman Catholic Church, since October 1984. A printed report of this dialogue, entitled *Journeying Together in Christ*, has been made available through Our Sunday Visitor in Huntington, Indiana, and I urge you all to get a copy. It's really interesting reading. And the report shows, that although obstacles remain, there's much convergence between us in doctrine, sacraments, devotion to Jesus and Mary, and Christian life.... The histories which I included in this report, one written by your representative and one by our representative, are very interesting. They indicate that both sides are responsible for the division which developed, not just one but both sides, and we, Roman Catholics, I'm telling you now, are sorry for the part we played in this division.

Following his return from Canada, Bishop Brzana remained in frequent contact with the NCCB's Committee for Ecumenical and Interreligious Affairs. On behalf of the PNCC-RC dialogue members, he had been coordinating efforts to petition Rome for a favorable decision regarding the applicability of Canon 844, n.3, of the 1983 Code of Canon Law. The issue was whether members of the PNCC could in certain circumstances receive the sacraments of penance, the Eucharist, and anointing of the sick. Canon 844, n.3, reads as follows:

Catholic ministers administer the sacraments of penance, Eucharist, and anointing of the sick licitly to members of Eastern Churches which do not have full communion with the Catholic Church if they seek such on their own accord and are properly disposed. This is also valid for members of other Churches which in the judgment of the Apostolic See are in the same condition in regard to the sacraments as these Eastern Churches.

This section of the Code of Canon Law became the focus of much discussion, analysis, and planning. The members of the dialogue early on had identified it as a critical means by which the shared understanding by the two churches of the sacraments of penance, Eucharist, and anointing of the sick could be expressed. During the PNCC National Clergy Conference on November 4-5, 1987, at All Saints Parish, Carnegie, Pennsylvania, the issue of intercommunion was first raised. After having received a report on the progress of the dialogue by Bishop Rysz, the clergy in attendance passed a resolution declaring "the desire on our part to further improve relationships between our two churches by establishing intercommunion."

The achievement of sacramental sharing between the two churches continued to be a goal that the members of the dialogue team earnestly sought. The responsibility for bringing this matter to the Apostolic See by way of the NCCB's Committee for Ecumenical and Interreligious Affairs was shared by Bishop Brzana and Father Hotchkin. During the latter part of 1990, the process continued in Washington, D.C., at the NCCB headquarters, and in Scranton, with consultation involving Prime Bishop Swantek.

The release of *Journeying Together in Christ* and the exploration of the applicability of Canon 844 were important developments during 1990. In addition, it should be noted that the PNCC-RC dialogue members also wanted to find ways to heal the division and the hurt that reached back almost one hundred years. The faithful in both churches had been impacted by the excommunication of Father Francis Hodur in 1898 by Bishop Michael J. Hoban. There was a growing awareness among the dialogue participants that a statement focusing on reconciliation and forgiveness would greatly aid the clergy and the laity of both churches, as together they sought to move beyond the pain and passions of the past. During the fall 1990 dialogue meeting at Stella Maris Retreat House, Skaneateles, New York, discussion about the language of a statement took place. It was agreed that both the RC participants and the members of the PNCC dialogue commission should prepare drafts. The drafts would then be studied at a later date.

In an April 4, 1991, letter, Archbishop Pilarczyk, the president of the NCCB, wrote to then Archbishop Edward I. Cassidy, head of the Pontifical Council for Promoting Christian Unity. Archbishop Pilarczyk wrote: "... in behalf of the National Conference of Catholic Bishops of the U.S.A., may I present the following question to the Apostolic See: Will the Pontifical Council for Promoting Christian Unity declare that the Polish National Catholic Church of North America is 'in the same condition as Oriental Churches' in this matter, and thus allow its members to receive the Sacraments of Penance, Eucharist, and Anointing of the Sick according to Canon 844, n.3?"

The question was able to be posed because the dialogue sessions had clearly identified key areas of agreement and had shown that the churches held the same belief about the sacraments in question. The sessions had produced an unprecedented agreement in such a short time. The formal talks began in 1984, and in less than ten years, a petition had made its way through the PNCC National Clergy Conference and the National Conference of Catholic Bishops to Rome. While the faithful of both churches were aware that sacramental sharing had been discussed during the dialogue sessions, few knew that the matter had moved beyond discussion stages to the point of decision.

Archbishop Cassidy replied in a May 21, 1991, letter to Archbishop Pilarczyk. He wrote, "Be assured that this Council wishes to support the very promising developments that have taken place between the National Conference of Catholic Bishops and the PNCC, including the stated goal of the dialogue, namely, contributing 'to the progress of all our people toward the great goal of unity' (*Journeying Together in Christ*, p. 35), a goal to which we believe Our Lord calls all of his disciples."

While he expressed the hope for future unity, Archbishop Cassidy indicated that the question posed by Archbishop Pilarczyk raised two concerns that necessarily had to be addressed by the council. He said that clarification was needed on two points: "Does the PNCC maintain relationships of sacramental sharing with other Churches or ecclesial communities? If so, which ones? Are there, in fact, clergy in the PNCC who had previously been ordained as Roman Catholic priests? If so, could you give us some details?"

In view of these questions, it became clear that there was more work to do. Responses would have to be sent to Archbishop Cassidy before any determination about the applicability of Canon 844 to the PNCC would be determined by the Holy See.

During the spring dialogue session, held on May 22-23, 1991, in Mississauga, Ontario, the response from Archbishop Cassidy was not yet known to the participants. Bishop Brzana felt the need to report to the group that Archbishop Pilarczyk's inquiry regarding Canon 844 had been submitted to the council headed by Archbishop Cassidy, who on June 28, 1991, was elevated to the College of Cardinals. Knowing that the members of the dialogue were eager to learn whether Rome would react favorably to the Canon 844 proposal, Bishop Brzana again made certain that the participants kept the issue in the forefront.

On May 27, 1991, Bishop Thaddeus Peplowski, Bishop of the PNCC's Buffalo-Pittsburgh Diocese and member of the dialogue team, traveled to Rome in an unofficial capacity and had a private audience with Pope John Paul II. In a written report summarizing the meeting, Bishop Peplowski observed: "The

Pontiff was well informed about the progress of the Dialogue and seemed pleased the way it is developing." The following day, the PNCC clergy met with the soon-to-be Cardinal Cassidy at his office in Rome. At that session, Bishop Peplowski learned that the proposal concerning Canon 844, n.3, had certainly gained the attention of the staff at the Council for Promoting Christian Unity. Again, according to a report of the meeting, it was observed by Bishop Peplowski that the president of the council "spoke with great enthusiasm regarding the petition recently sent to Rome from the NCCB regarding canon 844, paragraph 3. At this time Archbishop Cassidy stated that the petition has reached the Vatican; however, more information is needed before Rome can comment on the petition."

Journeying Together in Christ continued to generate interest among the laity and clergy in both churches. On September 23, 1991, a prayer service was held in Chicago to allow the faithful to "receive" the report of the PNCC-RC dialogue. The gathering was sponsored by the Archdiocese of Chicago and the Western Diocese of the PNCC. In attendance at the service were: Cardinal Joseph Bernardin, Prime Bishop Swantek, and Bishop Joseph Zawistowski, head of the PNCC Western Diocese, along with other members of the local clergy. Interest in the talks between the two churches brought together men and women who knew that praying for God's assistance was a necessary first step in achieving reconciliation and, possibly, unity.

At the November 6-7, 1991, dialogue session held in Scranton, the subject of a meeting with Cardinal Cassidy was raised by Bishop Timlin. What had been proposed by the president of the council was that he visit St. Stanislaus Polish National Catholic Cathedral in Scranton on Saturday, February 15, 1992. The objective was to communicate the Holy Father's personal interest in the progress of the dialogue and to encourage the faithful of both churches to continue to find what unites them. Father Senior Skrzypek, the ecumenical officer for the PNCC, said that he would ask Prime Bishop Swantek to extend an invitation to the Cardinal.

Since the fall meeting in 1990, the PNCC-RC dialogue participants had been working on drafts of statements that would address the pain and difficulties of the past and their hopes for the future. Before concluding the November 7, 1991, session, it was agreed that the goal was to have the statements ready as part of a prayer service that would be conducted when Cardinal Cassidy traveled to Scranton in 1992. Bishop Timlin and Bishop Rysz agreed to plan for the historic visit.

Scranton's *Sunday Times* of February 16, 1992, ran a front-page headline, "Churches Closer to Reunification." Those four words summed up the feelings of many who were present at the Service of Healing, which had taken place the day before, when Cardinal Cassidy carried a personal message from Pope John Paul II to a hopeful, joint congregation of the PNCC and RC faithful — one which had never before been assembled in Scranton.

The unprecedented gathering took place at noon, at St. Stanislaus Polish National Catholic Cathedral in South Scranton. Here on the original site of the establishment of the PNCC were gathered RC bishops; PNCC bishops and clergy and their parishioners; RC priests from neighboring parishes and members of their congregations; prominent lay leaders of the PNCC; two choirs — one from St. Stanislaus Cathedral and a choir from St. Aloysius Church in Wilkes-Barre, Pennsylvania. All of those assembled in Bishop Francis Hodur's venerable cathedral were earnestly seeking healing and reconciliation. All sensed that they were not only witnesses to history, but that they were also participants in a holy moment in the lives of the faithful of both churches.

Joining with Cardinal Cassidy were Prime Bishop Swantek, Bishop Rysz, and Bishop Peplowski for the PNCC. Representing the RC church were Bishop Brzana and Bishop Timlin from the dialogue team. They were joined by Bishop J. Carroll McCormick, retired Bishop of Scranton, and by Bishop Francis X. DiLorenzo, then the Auxiliary Bishop of Scranton. Some fifty members of the clergy were also in attendance, as well as a standing-room-only throng that actually spilled out of the cathedral.

Following the procession into the cathedral, Bishop Rysz offered welcoming remarks (for the complete text, see Appendix I — Document 1). He reflected on the origin of the PNCC and the division that resulted when two hundred fifty families gathered with Father Francis Hodur because "they sought to worship and work in the church which was their heritage, their Mother and guardian in the vicissitudes of their difficult life." Quoting from the introduction to *Journeying Together in Christ*, which he and Bishop Brzana had drafted, Bishop Rysz stressed that all the people in both churches had to take up the "arduous spiritual task of the purification of memory" so as not to be "encrusted with bitterness despite the pain all have felt."

After the opening prayer and the readings from Sacred Scripture, Bishop Brzana delivered the "Statement of Roman Catholic Bishops Engaged in Dialogue with the Polish National Catholic Bishops" (for the complete text, see Appendix I — Document 2). The RC bishops sought to place the break in Church unity within its historical context. They maintained, "The dispute was not over doctrine but over organizational matters." While they claimed there were no doctrinal issues that drove Father Hodur to organize the PNCC, the bishops recognized the strife that resulted in the riven faith communities. The bishops focused on the atmosphere during the late nineteenth century when the conflict arose: "Feeling ran very deep in those days. Many still remember the great hurt and the anguish experienced as families split over the dispute and neighborhood friends virtually became enemies. It is difficult for us to appreciate how painful were the wounds on both sides during those tumultuous times."

The bishops made it clear that they were also not eager to sit in judgment of Father Hodur's actions; rather, they wished to consider them only within their historical context when the break in Catholic unity occurred. The bishops stated: "It is understood that we should not attempt to rewrite history, nor should we judge the sincerity of the good people of those days. Neither can we pretend that these events were not what they were in that particularly troubled period of history. Those were difficult and trying days and no doubt the central figures in the dispute said and did what they thought to be just and proper under the circumstances."

Hoping to consign the harsh words and uncharitable behavior of the past to oblivion, the bishops offered a sincere apology to the clergy and faithful of the PNCC. The bishops declared, "We deeply regret, all the times, that we, their brothers and sisters in the Lord, have been insensitive or have offended them in any way."

After Bishop Brzana concluded, Bishop Rysz read the "Statement of Polish National Catholic Bishops Engaged in Dialogue with the Roman Catholic Bishops" (for the complete text, see Appendix I — Document 3). Those gathered in St. Stanislaus Cathedral were impressed by similarities in thinking and sentiment that were present in both statements. The PNCC bishops also emphasized that the origin of the conflict was not over doctrinal matters. They asserted, "The birth of the Polish National

Catholic Church was not due to matters of faith but rather over the administration of the temporalities of the church." They also focused on Father Hodur's efforts to "seek the help of the Holy Father in resolving the difficulties which arose in Scranton" and how he journeyed to Rome in 1898 toward that good end. Seeking to put the actions of the late nineteenth century within their historical context, while also not passing judgment on the participants in the religious conflict, the bishops stated: "Abuses were prevalent on both sides of the disputing parties. Painful as these abuses were, we recognize that each side acted in good faith and was convinced that it was doing God's will."

The desire to move away from the tribulations of the past was also evident in the PNCC bishops' statement. They, too, wanted to cast into oblivion the hurts and outrages of the past. However, the pain resulting from Francis Hodur's excommunication was alluded to when the bishops expressed the hope that he and others "who acted in accord with their conscience, be cleared of all allegations." In the end, the bishops were forward-looking and desirous of a future in which the two churches would work in harmony, with unity in Christ as the desired goal. Their statement was clear: "We extend the hand of love, friendship and fraternity to our brothers and sisters of the Roman Catholic Church." In another section of the statement, the bishops declared: "In recent years, we have met in ecumenical forums both locally and internationally which have testified to our mutual desire for unity in Christ."

After the singing of the traditional Polish hymn "Serdeczna Matko," Prime Bishop Swantek, as leader of the PNCC, delivered a Spiritual Address (for the complete text, see Appendix I — Document 4). He stressed the need to confront the churches' failures to live up to the tenets of the faith as outlined in the

Nicene Creed, which the faithful of both churches profess. He said that the failure to love as Jesus Christ did also had to be confronted. The Prime Bishop said: "It is very difficult to admit one's failings, for we all have a certain amount of pride as well as some blindness, but our Lord Jesus Christ is very much aware of how often we have failed Him, for we have acted in a sense at one time or another like Peter on the night that Christ was arrested. Through the things we said and did, we too denied that we knew Jesus."

Clearly, Prime Bishop Swantek's intention was to keep those in attendance focused on the purpose of the Service of Healing, which was an examination of conscience, so that real healing and reconciliation could take place.

Cardinal Cassidy was the next speaker at the Service of Healing. He read a personal message from Pope John Paul II, which was addressed to the Prime Bishop (for the complete text, see Appendix I — Document 5). The letter from the Pope, which was dated February 4, 1992, reported that he had great interest in the dialogue. Above all, the letter expressed hope for the future. Pope John Paul II wrote, "Through the dialogue and further steps taken recently, new hopes are raised that the events which some decades ago led to a break in the ecclesial unity which we had previously enjoyed can be put behind us, and that one day full communion in the one apostolic faith, sacramental life and mission, to which Christ calls us, can be restored."

This vision of the restoration of unity between the two churches may have been startling to some in attendance who were not aware of the great strides that had occurred in the dialogue sessions and in the meetings that had taken place in Rome.

Following the reading of the Pope's letter, Cardinal Cassidy delivered his own remarks (for the complete text, see Appendix I

— Document 6). The first part of his talk featured a careful analysis of the statements issued by the PNCC and RC bishops. He paid particular attention to the great similarities that were evident. He noted that both speakers maintained that there were no substantive doctrinal issues separating the churches, that both churches sought to consign the difficulties of the past to oblivion, and that the episcopal leadership earnestly sought reconciliation, harmony, and friendship for their clergy and laity.

Cardinal Cassidy's speech was much more than a commentary and critique of the statements that had been delivered by Bishop Brzana and Bishop Rysz. In the end, his talk was a powerful exhortation to continue on the journey to unity. Warning that "separation by its very nature creates a culture which always seeks to build on separation itself no matter what the original reasons for division were," the Cardinal pleaded for the continuation of meaningful dialogue that would produce reconciliation. He told those gathered in St. Stanislaus Cathedral that they had a unique opportunity to achieve the unity that Christ willed for His followers. Cardinal Cassidy asserted:

> [T]hrough dialogue and renewed contacts in recent years and today, with these statements of reconciliation, the Polish National Catholic Church and the Roman Catholic Church are taking serious steps to replace division, and the culture it produces, with a process of reconciliation. How urgent it is that this continue. And since neither side sees disputes in faith at the origin of their separation, how much more opportunity that seems to give for reconciliation.

The congregation that filled St. Stanislaus Cathedral had much to reflect on during the Service of Healing on February 15,

1992. Certainly, they had learned much about the progress of the dialogue sessions from the report set forth in *Journeying Together in Christ*. On that Saturday afternoon in South Scranton, the clergy and laity of both churches experienced the power of God's grace when Bishop Timlin led the congregation in offering a sign of peace. It seemed that the divisions of decades melted away as the choir sang "One Bread, One Body," while bishops, priests, and laity of both churches embraced or extended hands in friendship.

The words spoken in St. Stanislaus Cathedral drew attention in both the secular and the religious press. *The New York Times* carried a story on the Service of Healing in its Monday (February 17, 1992) edition. *Catholic New York*, in a February 27, 1992, editorial, observed: "The aura of faith and charity that filled the cathedral was a far cry from the bitterness that marked the riot leading to the founding of the Polish church. It happened nearly 100 years ago, at a time when national concerns and sensitivities were issues of major proportion — and when strongly willed religious leaders were likely to take forceful stands that left little room for retreat or compromise."

Both *The Catholic Light*, the Scranton diocesan newspaper, and *God's Field*, the biweekly of the PNCC, published the complete texts of the statements that the PNCC and RC bishops delivered during the historic gathering. The texts, along with Cardinal Cassidy's statement, were circulated in the Catholic News Service Documentary Service, *Origins*, of February 27, 1992. Every RC bishop in the United States had an opportunity to learn what had taken place in Scranton at St. Stanislaus Cathedral.

After the Service of Healing in Scranton, a similar gathering was held on March 29 in the PNCC's Holy Mother of the Rosary Cathedral in Buffalo. During that service, Bishop Peplowski and Bishop Edward Head of the Diocese of Buffalo signed a covenant in which they pledged to foster between the churches "ongoing dialogue, mutual respect and concern, sharing of devotional services, and cooperation in matters concerning our community." *God's Field*, in the April 25, 1992, edition, reported on the ceremony:

> Perhaps the most "heart wrenching" portion of this Ecumenical Service was in the introduction of the "Sign of Peace," offered by Bishop Rysz. After nearly 100 years of conflict and discontent, the Bishop, clergy, and congregation offered each other the sign of peace, with embraces, handshakes and hugs, with many tears following unshameably from the participants. Many of the congregants [were] saying, "What a wonderful feeling this is," and "This should have happened many years ago. . . ."

The dialogue team knew that there was still much work to be done if the two churches were to continue on the journey to unity. The next dialogue session was scheduled for June 3-4, 1992, in Buffalo. During the spring session, there was a status report concerning the applicability of Canon 844, n. 3. The participants learned that the petition to have the PNCC placed in the same condition as the Eastern churches with regard to the sacraments of penance, Eucharist, and anointing of the sick was before the Congregation for the Doctrine of the Faith in Rome.

Following Services of Healing in Scranton and Buffalo, there was another sign that relations between the PNCC and the RC churches were improving. On June 12-13, 1992, two RC priests gave a retreat at the Bishop Hodur Retreat and Recreation Center, Waymart, Pennsylvania. The retreat was sponsored by the Fellowship of Saint John the Evangelist, a PNCC society that fosters prayer life for both the clergy and laity. About fifty persons gathered at the center to hear from Monsignor John Esseff and Father Leo McKernan, the director of ecumenism for the Diocese of Scranton. *God's Field* (July 4, 1992, edition) reported on the gathering:

> The retreat was held to spiritually nourish and strengthen interested people of the diocese. It also served to better ecumenical relations between Polish National Catholics and Roman Catholics. All those who attended the retreat saw it as a "time of grace" in which the Holy Spirit was present. All agreed that such events are needed to take place more frequently in our church.

During the fall dialogue session, October 28-29, 1992, in Boston, the participants again focused on Canon 844, n.3. Bishop Brzana informed those present that he expected a reply from the Congregation for the Doctrine of the Faith before Christmas. But the reply would not come until the following spring.

Relations between the RC and PNCC continued to warm during the early part of 1993, when clergy from both churches took part in one of Catholicism's most venerable Lenten observances, the Stations of the Cross. On Wednesday, March 24, Father Joseph Quinn, rector of St. Peter's Cathedral, Scranton, and Father Joseph Bambera, director of ecumenism for the Diocese of Scranton, joined Bishop Rysz and Father Charles Csirip, assistant pastor at St. Stanislaus Cathedral, in praying the Stations in the PNCC cathedral. The following Friday, March 26, Father Csirip and Father Senior Francis Kolwicz, vice-rector of Savonarola Theological Seminary, Scranton, participated in the

Stations of the Cross conducted at St. Peter's Cathedral. Bishop Rysz commented on the significance of the joint experience of the Lenten prayer service: "Our mutual sharing of this Lenten tradition is not just a symbolic gesture. I truly see it as a powerful sign of our commitment to the necessary spiritual cooperation to which the Gospel calls us. By showing a mutual respect for our individual traditions, we would be laying the necessary foundation on which we can build our future shared worshipping experiences."

"Shared worshipping experiences" were the subject of the March 29, 1993, letter that Cardinal Cassidy wrote to Archbishop William Keeler, who had succeeded Archbishop Pilarczyk as president of the National Conference of Catholic Bishops. Rome had finally replied to the petition concerning Canon 844, which had first been presented in April 1991. The message was favorable. Cardinal Cassidy wrote:

> This request was forwarded, with a recommendation for favourable consideration, to the Congregation for the Doctrine of the Faith for its judgment. In so doing, we pointed out the background motivation for this petition, including the pastoral aspect, namely that because the PNCC is concentrated in certain parts of the United States, its faithful in other areas of the country do not have normal access to their own priests. We also noted that over the last decade an important dialogue has been in progress between the Polish National Catholic Church and the Roman Catholic Church, whose recent report (*Journeying Together in Christ*) has shown a significant convergence on fundamental theological questions and the desire for reconciliation.

Archbishop Keeler immediately notified the chairman of the NCCB's Committee for Ecumenical and Interreligious Affairs, Archbishop Rembert G. Weakland, O.S.B., of the decision by the Holy See. On April 16, 1993, Archbishop Weakland wrote to all bishops in the United States and alerted them to the new application of Canon 844, n.3. He succinctly explained the implications of the decision to his brother bishops: "In behalf of the Holy See, Cardinal Edward Cassidy wrote to Archbishop Keeler on March 29, 1993, indicating the judgment of the Holy See is affirmative; Polish National Catholics do come under the provision of Canon 844, n.3. This means that we may administer the three sacraments to Polish National Catholics who request them of us and are rightly disposed, requiring no more of them than we would of Roman Catholics."

The spring dialogue session took place on April 21-22, 1993, at Our Savior Polish National Catholic Church, Dearborn Heights, Michigan. Bishop Brzana read Cardinal Cassidy's March 29, 1993, letter to the participants. Bishop Rysz, speaking for the PNCC, said that the response from Rome was most welcome news. Both sides agreed that a press release would have to be prepared so that the clergy and faithful in both churches would know of the Holy See's decision. The release would also have to address the questions about implementation that were sure to arise. Bishop Timlin volunteered to prepare a draft of the release. This draft was reviewed by the dialogue teams, and the press release was prepared for dissemination on April 29, 1993. The statement was to be released in Washington, D.C.

Entitled "Joint Statement Issued by the Members of the Polish National Catholic Church-Roman Catholic Church Dialogue After Their Meeting on April 22, 1993, in Dearborn Heights, Michigan," the statement sought to provide a brief narrative of how the question of sacramental sharing with the PNCC came about (for the complete text, see Appendix I — Document 7). In addition, the statement quoted Canon 844 in its entirety so that those unfamiliar with the 1983 Code of Canon Law would have an opportunity to read the applicable statute.

Catholic New Service asked Father Hotchkin, dialogue participant and executive director of the NCCB's Secretariat for Ecumenical and Interreligious Affairs, about the decision. CNS reported that he indicated that "the decision could have significant impact for Polish National Catholics because it offers them access to Mass and the sacraments when travel or work takes them to the many parts of the country where their own church has no priests or parishes."

Also released with the Dearborn Heights statement was an official response from the PNCC dialogue commission (for the complete text, see Appendix I — Document 8). The statement was positive, joyful, and forward-looking. The commission members stated: "The clarification regarding the opportunity to receive the sacraments of Penance, Eucharist and Anointing of the Sick, under certain conditions strengthens those fraternal ties which already exist. We trust that, under the guidance of the Holy Spirit, we may collaborate on developing guidelines which will increase our opportunities for pastoral care and a common witness."

While the Dearborn Heights statement was officially disseminated from Washington, D.C., there were releases in other locales where interest in the progress of the dialogue would be valued. On April 29, 1993, Bishop Timlin met with Bishop Rysz at St. Stanislaus Cathedral. They posed for a photograph to mark the significant development in the PNCC-RC dialogue. *The Scranton Times* on Friday, April 30, 1993, carried a front-page banner headline, "Two Churches Improve Relations." Later, the same newspaper editorialized on the major breakthrough. In the following Thursday edition (May 6, 1993), the editors asserted that it was indeed "splendid news" that the dialogue had produced improved relations between the churches; moreover, they believed this would surely translate into the strengthening of the community as a whole.

The fall dialogue sessions were held on October 27-28, 1993, in Hartford, Connecticut. The clergy from both churches gathered for the celebration of Mass and, for the first time since the start of the dialogue in 1984, PNCC participants received the Holy Eucharist from the RC celebrant. In addition to the exploration of possible models of how unity between the two churches could be achieved, the dialogue members discussed the pressing need to develop guidelines that would aid PNCC and RC clergy and laity in the reception of the sacraments of penance, Eucharist, and anointing of the sick. The topic of the guidelines had arisen previously at the Dearborn Heights, Michigan, gathering, and it was determined that Father Hotchkin and Father Senior Skrzypek, the PNCC ecumenical officer, would work on the guidelines. In Hartford, the issue again had to be addressed.

With a draft of the guidelines on hand, Father Hotchkin said that it would have to be reviewed by the NCCB's Administrative Board. He proposed that this be placed before that body in March 1994, when they were scheduled to meet. Similarly, the PNCC bishops would have an opportunity to study the proposed guidelines at their next conference.

There was only one dialogue session during 1994 because in the fall of the year Bishop Timlin had been called to Rome to attend a synod on the consecrated life. On April 21-22, at the chancery of the PNCC Central Diocese in Scranton, the members of the dialogue team again focused on the guidelines associated with the implementation of Canon 844, n.3. The language of the canon clearly indicated that members of Oriental churches — and now, by approval of the Holy See, members of the PNCC — could receive the sacraments of penance, Eucharist, and anointing of the sick "if they ask on their own for the sacraments and are properly disposed." The guidelines under consideration had stipulations that some on the dialogue team found needlessly wordy (for the complete text, see Appendix I — Document 9). Father Senior Skrzypek asserted that they would highlight "a sense of disunity." Indeed, the guidelines were very clear about which members of the PNCC church could seek the sacraments from a RC priest:

> The decision applies to members in good standing of the Polish National Catholic Church who are not otherwise individually impeded by canonical sanction of the Roman Catholic Church. This restriction would apply to those individuals who once were Roman Catholics and incurred a sanction which has not subsequently been lifted by the Roman Catholic Church. Such, for instance, would be the case of a Roman Catholic priest who set aside his priestly obligations without a dispensation. Others might be impeded from receiving the Eucharist because of their marital situation.

The members of the dialogue teams knew that when they adjourned from the spring sessions that there needed to be study and consultation regarding the guidelines. That the language of the document was already widely circulated became apparent at the Nineteenth General Synod of the PNCC, which took place on October 10-14, 1994, in Buffalo. Bishop Rysz presented a report on the activities and achievements of the dialogue commission during the fourth session on October 13, 1994.

Following his report, then Very Rev. Casimir Grotnik rose to address the assembly. He announced that he was "speaking on behalf of thirty-eight former Roman Catholic priests who are currently working in our Polish National Catholic Church. And on behalf of many of our parishioners, former Roman Catholics, who freely joined this beautiful democratic Church." The priest went on to quote the section of the guidelines set forth above. He labeled the paragraph "discriminatory and divisive of the clergy and faithful as well." In his view, "it does not contribute to the main goal of the dialogue, the unity of the church." According to the transcript of the Buffalo gathering, Very Rev. Grotnik's remarks received "applause from the Synodal Body."

Bishop Rysz responded by reading from a letter that he had sent to all of the priests of the PNCC Central Diocese after their meeting on September 27, 1994. The Bishop stressed that, in all matters, he and the other members of the dialogue commission had been open and frank. He said that the guidelines associated with Canon 844 had been shared with all of the bishops. Bishop Rysz then offered his understanding of the meaning of the canon and the applicability of the guidelines as they relate to former Roman Catholic priests:

> Canon 844.3 does not address any matter of unity. It does not in any way approve or foresee any concelebrations, whether with former Roman Catholic priests or for that matter with priests baptized, raised and educated in institutions of the Polish National Catholic Church. All it does is treat the PNCC as it does the Oriental Churches

which allows Polish National Catholics to receive the Sacraments of Penance, Communion and Anointing in the absence of their own priest on the same conditions as those are received by Roman Catholics in their own Church.

Every Roman Catholic priest is totally aware of the sanction placed upon him by his Church, when he chooses to break the law which he promised to uphold when he was ordained. Bishop Hodur and the organizers of the Polish National Catholic Church knew and understood this. Once they decided that the Canon Law of the Roman Catholic Church no longer bound them in conscience or in fact they never let it interfere in the work which they undertook for the Gospel of the Lord and for His Church. They also were totally unconcerned with the reception of Sacraments in the Roman Catholic Church because they never doubted the validity of the Sacraments in their own.

Every Roman Catholic priest is also aware that he automatically incurs excommunication when he attempts to marry. This is Roman Catholic law. There's nothing the PNCC Commission can do to change this. Since the PNCC allows its priests to marry, this matter was never an impediment to the exercise of the priestly ministry in the PNCC.

Clearly, the guidelines were problematic for many in attendance at the Nineteenth General Synod. Prime Bishop Swantek said that the exclusions from the sacraments were difficult to accept. He asked the members of the PNCC dialogue commission to continue to focus on them in order that "healing and forgiveness be manifested between two Christian bodies." Asserting that the guidelines would have a telling impact on real people, the Prime Bishop said: "When I read the guidelines, I think of someone very close to me who would also be within that excluded group. And so, I would address the Dialogue Committee that at the next meeting, when they review those with the Roman Catholic Church, that they concentrate on being able to see what can be done, if anything can be."

The next meeting of the PNCC-RC dialogue team took place in Scranton at the RC chancery on May 17-18, 1995. Again, the guidelines for Canon 844 were a key item on the agenda. While it was clear that there were many members of the clergy and laity of the PNCC who were seeking the removal of the language dealing with the "restrictions" set forth in the guidelines, it was very evident to all of the participants in the dialogue that a major hurdle had been encountered in the matter of RC priests and lay people who had knowingly departed the RC Church.

In 1991, when then Archbishop Cassidy responded to the initial petition from the president of the NCCB that the PNCC be considered in the same condition as the Oriental churches, he directly touched on the notion of priests who had abandoned the RC Church for the Old Catholic Church. His May 21, 1991, letter to Archbishop Pilarczyk stated the following:

> ... having in mind the fact that there are former Catholic priests among the Old Catholic clergy, this Council inquired of the Congregation for the Doctrine of the Faith whether it was admissible for Catholics to ask the sacraments from Old Catholics who were former Roman Catholic clergy. The response was clearly negative. The

reasoning was that, just as Catholic priests who have been dispensed are prohibited from every exercise of sacred orders, such prohibition would apply for greater reason and serious pastoral motives for priests ordained in the Catholic Church who are no longer in communion with the Roman Catholic Church. Catholic faithful, therefore, should not seek the sacraments from them. I recognize that your petition concerns only Canon 844, n.3, but because of the natural desire to seek and to offer reciprocity in ecumenical relationships it seems important to be aware of this problem as well.

As problematic and potentially divisive as some might view them, the guidelines continued to be studied by the PNCC and RC clergy and in appropriate deliberative bodies. At the 1995 spring dialogue session, Bishop Timlin informed the participants that the guidelines had been placed before the NCCB's Committee for Ecumenical and Interreligious Affairs. On March 13, 1996, the chairman of the committee, Bishop Oscar Lipscomb, wrote to all RC bishops to inform them that the guidelines had been approved and that he was authorized to promulgate them. His letter provided background information about Canon 844, n. 3, and how approval for its application had been made to Rome. In addition, Bishop Lipscomb described the consultation that had occurred with the PNCC bishops and the implementation of the guidelines within the context of the 1993 Ecumenical Directory. The directory revised and expanded the norms on ecumenism published in 1967 and 1970, which the RC Church developed in response to Vatican II and the church's pledge to work tirelessly for Christian unity. The Bishop wrote:

As a next step, we then brought word of this clarification to the Polish National Catholic bishops who meet with us in ongoing dialogue, now co-chaired for us by Bishop James C. Timlin. Bishop Alfred Abramowicz, Bishop Alfred Markiewicz and Bishop Edward Grosz have also participated in these meetings on our behalf. We did this in keeping with what is set forth in the 1993 Ecumenical Directory, n. 130, directing that there be "consultation with at least the local competent authority of the other interested Church or ecclesial Community." As a result of these consultations, the bishops of our Churches worked together to develop mutually acceptable guidelines for the admission of Polish National Catholics to sacraments in the Roman Catholic Church. These have been favorably reviewed by the Committee for Ecumenical and Interreligious Affairs acting in consultation with the Pontifical Council for Promoting Christian Unity.

As the dialogue sessions continued during the next six years, the participants always returned to the issue of the reception of the sacraments, as well as the status of former RC priests and lay men and women who had left the RC Church to join the PNCC. While respect for the traditions and practices of each church was always a given since the dialogue commenced in 1984, the two churches, despite the profession of respect, understood all too clearly that unity had not been achieved. The guidelines that were disseminated in 1996 recognized that the separation remained, yet there was always the expression of a deep and abiding hope. The guidelines concluded: "Regrettably our churches are still divided. But we do hope that the clarification we have received from Rome will advance our churches toward that full communion of faith and life that is both Christ's promise and His will for us. At the same time we trust it will be a source of pastoral and sacramental support for our people as they live out their faith."

In 1997, the PNCC marked the one hundredth anniversary of its establishment. The most solemn gathering of the centenary year was at St. Stanislaus Cathedral on March 9, 1997. Coming together were PNCC clerical and lay leaders from the United States and Canada, as well as numerous bishops and clerics from Old Catholic churches in Europe, including the Archbishop of Utrecht, the Most Rev. Antonius Glazemaker. Also in attendance were a number of RC priests and Bishop Timlin, who was invited to speak at the anniversary Mass.

The homily was delivered by Bishop Rysz, who reflected on the great hardships and pains that the founding members of the PNCC experienced as they began their faith journey one hundred years earlier. The Bishop reflected on the animosities that arose between members of the RC faith and Father Francis Hodur's followers. He said there was "a long period of divisions in families, discrimination and hatred that has persisted practically through our own day." Pointing to the ecumenical activity that has taken place between the two churches, Bishop Rysz said there is a new spirit of tolerance and reaching out.

Following the homily, Bishop Timlin spoke from the pulpit of St. Stanislaus Cathedral. For many, it was a remarkable sight: the successor to the RC bishop who had excommunicated Father Francis Hodur speaking in the place from which the PNCC had come into being. Earlier in 1997, on January 23, during the annual observance of the Week of Prayer for Christian Unity, Prime Bishop Swantek became the first PNCC prelate to speak from the pulpit of St. Peter's Cathedral. That doors which once were barred were now thrown open was a source of joy among the clergy and laity of both churches.

Bishop Timlin delivered a pastoral letter to those gathered at St. Stanislaus Cathedral (for the complete text, see Appendix I — Document 10). He begged forgiveness for the sins of the past, and he pledged that he would work for unity. He said: ". . . with profound sorrow I beg your forgiveness for every offense, mis-understanding, unkind act, mistaken judgment, or any other thought, word, or deed ever committed against you through prej-udice, thoughtlessness, or suspicious misgivings on the part of anyone in the Roman Catholic community. And I pledge on the occasion of this meaningful anniversary that my desire, as long as I live, will be to ever strive to restore the unity that was once ours so that our nearness purchased by the blood of Christ will be all he intended it to be."

Bishop Timlin's pastoral letter was published in the April 3, 1997, issue of *Origins* as well as in Our Sunday Visitor's bimonthly *The Catholic Answer.* There was widespread praise for the message he communicated. Seeking forgiveness and pledging to work for unity, though, seemed to echo much of what had been spoken of five years earlier when Cardinal Cassidy had come to Scranton and conveyed to the clergy and laity of the PNCC and RC that Pope John Paul II had taken a personal interest in the dialogue and had been praying for its success. But after five years, many of the faithful in both churches were unfamiliar with the progress of the talks. Those who followed the rather brief press releases that were issued at the conclusion of each session really did not know much about the substance of the theological and practical matters that were being discussed by the participants in the dialogue.

Following the centennial observance in 1997, the dialogue participants continued to search for some way to bring about reciprocity so that the RC faithful could receive the sacraments from PNCC clergy. This lack of reciprocity was a very sensitive issue among many of the PNCC faithful. Participants in the dialogue frequently asserted that it made some members of the clergy and laity feel confused by the "one-sided" or "discriminatory" guidelines that were promulgated in 1996.

In an effort to see whether reciprocity could be achieved, Bishop Timlin wrote to Archbishop Alexander Brunett, chairman of the NCCB's Committee for Ecumenical and Interreligious Affairs, on January 12, 1998. His letter addressed "the matters such as reciprocity in regard to the sacraments, and the questions of acting as godparents, and the requirements of canonical form for lawfulness only in mixed marriages. . . ." A response to this inquiry was reported at the October 24-25, 2001, dialogue session. The Administrative Board of the NCCB indicated it was not the opportune time to go beyond what was presented in the guidelines promulgated in 1996. Moreover, it was asserted that Roman Catholics could receive the sacraments in Polish National Catholic Churches "according to the norms" already in place. Catholic News Service reported on the announcement after the fall dialogue session: "Bishop Timlin informed the group that upon further consultation the Catholic bishops' committee felt sufficient guidance for Catholics already exists in the church's Code of Canon Law and 1993 Ecumenical Directory, so the project of specific Roman Catholic-PNCC guidelines should not go forward. The bishops have not developed comparable guidelines on when U.S. Catholics may receive sacraments that the Catholic Church recognizes as valid in other Christian churches."

While it was true that the dialogue had produced a significant achievement — the admission of the PNCC faithful to the sacraments of penance, Eucharist, and anointing of the sick in RC churches — there were no "breakthroughs" after the 1993 decision regarding Canon 844 that the average person in the pew experienced. Following the historic Service of Healing in 1992 and the Dearborn Heights announcement, there was such hope and enthusiasm for ecumenical discussions and gatherings. In the years that followed, in the opinion of some observers, there seemed to be a diminution in the "passion for unity." This perception was not accurate, however. What was occurring in the dialogue sessions, and what continues to this very day, is serious analysis and study of very significant questions: What is the role of the Pope? What happens to the PNCC's organizational structures if there is linkage with the RC church? Why isn't there reciprocity between the two churches so that Roman Catholics can receive the Eucharist in a Polish National Catholic Church?

At the time of the Service of Healing in 1992, much was made of the assertion that there did not appear to be any significant doctrinal issues separating the two churches. The dialogue participants continued to voice the claim, and this happy conclusion did circulate among the faithful. However, if there were no disagreements concerning the tenets of the Catholic faith, there were significant differences that surfaced during the dialogue sessions concerning the role and authority of the Pope and what models of unity would actually permit the PNCC to forge a new relationship with the RC church without forsaking its own structures, practices, and the traditions that had developed over one hundred years. The RC side was faced with the problem posed by former Roman Catholic clerics and laity, who, by Canon Law, were excommunicated for knowingly breaking communion with the church. Finding the way to the unity that Christ willed for His followers was not as simple as many thought it would be in the early 1990s.

To exemplify this point and to understand the kind of discussions that took place in the semiannual dialogue sessions, it is instructive to consider how the essential concept of unity was approached by those participating in the talks. Father Senior Marcell W. Pytlarz, a member of the PNCC dialogue team, prepared a paper for the spring session that was held in Scranton on April 20-21, 1998. The centennial celebration that had been observed the previous year made it abundantly clear to the members of the PNCC that they had traveled a long way since Father Hodur accepted a call to serve as pastor of the church erected by the independent-minded men and women who separated from Sacred Hearts of Jesus and Mary Parish in South Scranton. In his paper entitled "Unity with Autonomy and Identity," Father Senior Pytlarz stressed the importance of what occurred in the life of the PNCC during the period 1897-1997. He wrote: "A hundred years is time for five generations to grow and mature. Historical processes seem vitally related to the demand for identity in each new generation. Time heals the wounds, but it also presents an opportunity for a community of people to develop its own identity. The traditional values become significant, new loyalties fuse with each other in a new sense of sameness and continuity."

Given the distinctive identity that had developed within the PNCC, Father Pytlarz argued that the challenge before the dialogue team was to find the path that would restore unity without depriving the PNCC of its historic achievements and its unique place in the Catholic family. Reaffirming the PNCC's Catholic roots and its own identity, Father Senior Pytlarz stressed, "While recognizing the primacy of the Bishop of Rome, the PNCC seeks equality, affirmation of the autonomous Church structures, self-governance, preservation of the cherished customs, practices, and ecclesial traditions."

On the RC side, there was certainly profound respect for the rich spirituality of the PNCC faithful and for the institutional achievements that had developed over the years. According to RC beliefs, such diversity and autonomy do not necessarily contradict the primacy of the Bishop of Rome, who has full and supreme teaching, governmental, and sacerdotal powers. His is a primacy of governance over the whole of Jesus' flock.

The question remains: How can the PNCC retain its autonomy, its own system of governance, and at the same time be united to the Bishop of Rome, who holds immediate jurisdiction over the entire Church? It is a complicated question, to be sure. Achieving unity, which is the holy objective of the dialogue sessions, remains a challenge for all who continue to hear the prayer of Jesus Christ that "all may be one" (Jn 17:21).

The PNCC held its Twentieth General Synod in Chicago during October 5-9, 1998. At the gathering, those in attendance approved "Guidelines for the Reception by Polish National Catholics of Sacraments in the Roman Catholic Church" (for the complete text, see Appendix I — Document 11). These guidelines were initially prepared by the Church Doctrine Commission. They also gained acceptance by the PNCC Bishops Conference. So that the membership of the entire church would have an opportunity to study them, the guidelines were published in *God's Field*. The PNCC faithful were advised that they could receive the sacraments of penance, Holy Eucharist, and anointing of the sick when they did not have access to their own clergy. Among other elements in the guidelines, the document contained specifics about the reception of Holy Communion in RC churches. It was viewed by the faithful as an educational document that addressed many of the concerns the clergy and laity of the PNCC had about the sacramental sharing that was a product of the PNCC-RC dialogue.

During the Twentieth General Synod, Bishop Rysz had the opportunity to deliver a comprehensive report on the developments that occurred in the PNCC-RC dialogue since the last synod. Having served as the co-chairman of the dialogue since its inception in 1984, Bishop Rysz brought a wealth of information to the assembly.

In what would be his final report on the talks between the PNCC and RC churches, he reminded the delegates to the synod that ecumenism had always been an important value for the PNCC. The Bishop focused on the earliest actions of Bishop Hodur and his outreach to other churches. Bishop Rysz said: "The Polish National Catholic Church, from its first Synod held in 1904, had gone on record to enter into cordial and friendly relations with other churches. Our first real encounter in ecumenical activity was the approach made by Father Franciszek Hodur regarding his consideration by the Church of Utrecht, Holland; and through this consecration making the PNCC an integral part of the churches of Catholic and apostolic tradition which did not accept Roman Catholic jurisdiction."

Bishop Rysz participated in only one other dialogue session, the November 4-5, 1998, gathering at the RC chancery in Scranton. In 1999, Bishop Rysz retired as Bishop of the Central Diocese. His was a long and valued tenure on the dialogue commission. Equally committed to the search for unity was Bishop Brzana, who had served as co-chairman with Bishop Rysz. He had retired from the See of Ogdensburg on November 11, 1993, when Bishop Timlin succeeded him as the RC co-chairman. Replacing Bishop Rysz as the PNCC's co-chairman in 1999 was Bishop Robert M. Nemkovich of the Western Diocese, who was elected Prime Bishop in 2002.

While the dialogue sessions — with their full agendas of theological questions and concerns — could be viewed as challenging for all involved, developments on the outside also made their way to the table. These issues often highlighted the fact that the churches still had many differences to bridge. For example, on November 30, 1999, two former RC priests, Father Senior Casimir Grotnik and Father Jan Dawidziuk, were consecrated bishops in St. Stanislaus Cathedral. No RC representative attended this significant event in the life of the PNCC community, although invitations had been extended. Again, the problem of former RC priests and their status in the PNCC came to the surface in a very public way.

Particularly problematic and painful to the PNCC side was the June 9, 2000, "reordination" of Father Jerzy Sieczynski by Auxiliary Bishop Patrick J. Zurek of the Archdiocese of San Antonio. Father Sieczynski had been ordained to the presbyterate on February 1, 1989, by Prime Bishop Swantek. He was suspended by the PNCC and sought admittance to the RC church. Labeled a mistake and a misunderstanding, the action by the Auxiliary Bishop brought to the forefront a question about the validity of the orders in the PNCC that had long ago been settled.

Also problematic for PNCC participants in the dialogue and among the members of the wider church community was the publication of *Dominus Iesus: On the Unicity and Salvific Universality of Jesus Christ and the Church.* Issued September 5, 2000, by the Vatican Congregation for the Doctrine of the Faith, the document advanced as truth "that the universal salvific will of the one and triune God is offered and accomplished once for all in the mystery of the incarnation, death, and resurrection of the Son of God." Further, *Dominus Iesus* also asserted that "there exists a single church of Christ, which subsists in the Catholic Church, governed by the successor of Peter and by the bishops in communion with him." From the RC point of view, the document simply reiterated the centrality of Jesus Christ in salvation history and the role of the Church He founded. Pope John Paul II sought to clarify the purpose of *Dominus Iesus* during a midday Angelus blessing service on October 1, 2000. He said, "The document clarifies essential Christian elements, which do not hinder dialogue but show its bases, because a dialogue without foundations would be destined to degenerate into empty wordiness."

Despite the clarifications and the efforts to put the document within a context, *Dominus Iesus* produced consternation and confusion among many who were involved in dialogues with the RC church. Certainly, that was the case when the fall dialogue session took place on October 24-25, 2000, at the PNCC National Church Center in Scranton. Prime Bishop Swantek requested that the document be placed on the agenda because it had created so much misunderstanding, hurt, and confusion, not only among the participants in the PNCC-RC dialogue, but among the faithful of many Christian congregations and other world religions. *Dominus Iesus* was discussed at that time, and its purpose and meaning continue to be of interest and concern for all those participating in ecumenical activity.

The election of former RC priests as PNCC bishops, the Sieczynski "reordination," and the release of *Dominus Iesus* by the Vatican stirred in some quarters the old suspicions, the distrust that was supposed to have been consigned to the past. Always, the members of the dialogue commission tried to find ways to express in one voice to the clergy and laity of both churches that hope for unity is ever present, that they will continue to use the sessions to find common ground, to identify what unites rather than focus on what differences remain.

C. S. Lewis, in the Preface to *Mere Christianity*, his beloved classic on Christian faith, maintained that the followers of Jesus have the ability to move beyond their differences, to find the core beliefs that all Christians share. Of Christianity, he wrote:

> It is at her centre, where her truest children dwell, that each communion is really closest to every other in spirit, if not in doctrine. And this suggests that at the centre of each there is something, or a Someone, who against all divergences of belief, all differences of temperament, all memories of mutual persecution, speaks with the same voice.

Finding that "same voice" remains the task before the PNCC-RC dialogue commission. It is true that the minutes of the dialogue for the last five years disclose that the unity which seemed almost imminent in1993 is not on the horizon. While the unity that Jesus Christ prayed for on the night before His death has not been achieved, the two churches will continue on the journey. The faithful of both churches continue to pray that some day they may find the "same voice" to worship as one the God who has bestowed blessings beyond measure upon all who call on Him.

JAMES B. EARLEY
Chancellor
Diocese of Scranton

Appendix I: Documents

Introduction

This section of the book contains a number of documents that were produced at various times for our dialogue during the years that this volume covers. These documents, which deal with a number of different topics of dialogue, appear in chronological order. They allow us to see how the work of dialogue has borne fruit in the lives of the faithful of our churches. We have included these materials in order that those interested in the work of dialogue between our churches may read for themselves the documents and speeches that were delivered to the faithful of both churches as they gathered together.

Documents 1 through 6 were presented during the time of the Service of Healing that was held on February 15, 1992, at St. Stanislaus Cathedral, the first parish of the Polish National Catholic Church. At this service, the bishops of the Roman Catholic Church, together with Edward Cardinal Cassidy, president of the Pontifical Council for Promoting Christian Unity, and the bishops of the Polish National Catholic Church, along with Prime Bishop John F. Swantek, together with a large number of clergy and laity of both churches, addressed each other and, more importantly, prayed with each other. These documents are preserved herein as an important record of this historic event within this dialogue.

Documents 7 through 9 were presented during the announcement of the extension of the courtesy of Canon 844.3 to Polish

National Catholics. This includes the official announcement of the sacramental sharing that exists between our churches as given by the bishops of the dialogue, and also the response of the Polish National Catholic bishops to the Vatican announcement of the extension of Canon 844.3 to the Polish National Catholic Church. We have included here a copy of the guidelines that govern the admission of Polish National Catholics to the sacraments of penance, Eucharist, and anointing of the sick within the Roman Catholic Church. Not included here is the statement of paragraph 123 of the 1993 Ecumenical Directory, which, under certain conditions, admits Roman Catholics to receive these same sacraments from the ministers of the Polish National Catholic Church.

Document 10 is the message of Bishop James C. Timlin, Roman Catholic Bishop of the Diocese of Scranton, to the bishops, clergy, and laity of the Polish National Catholic Church gathered at Holy Mass, in March 1997, for the celebration of the one hundredth anniversary of the organization of the Polish National Catholic Church. This message in many ways shows that in a short time our dialogue has brought us very far.

Lastly, Document 11 is the "Guidelines for the Reception by Polish National Catholics of Sacraments in the Roman Catholic Church." These guidelines were issued by the Church Doctrine Commission of the Polish National Catholic Church in response to the extension of the courtesy of Canon 844.3 to Polish National Catholics. In this document, the Polish National Catholic Church sets down norms for its faithful to receive the sacraments of Eucharist, penance, and anointing of the sick from ministers of the Roman Catholic Church. It also mentions that in the view of the Polish National Catholic Church, the faithful of the Roman Catholic Church should not be impeded from receiving these same sacraments from the ministers of the Polish National Catholic Church.

REV. ANTHONY A. MIKOVSKY
Representative of the PNCC-RC Dialogue

Document 1

Welcoming Remarks by Most Rev. Anthony M. Rysz

(Delivered at the Service of Healing, St. Stanislaus Polish National Catholic Cathedral, February 15, 1992)

Grace to you and peace from God the Father and our Lord Jesus Christ, who gave himself for our sins to deliver us from the present evil age, according to the will of our God and Father; to whom be the glory forever and ever. Amen. (Gal. 1:3–5)

With Paul's words of greeting to the churches of Galatia, I extend a cordial welcome to you who are gathered here in this historic church on this historical occasion: Your Grace, Most Reverend Prime Bishop Swantek; Bishop Thaddeus Peplowski; Your Eminence, Cardinal Cassidy; Your Excellencies, Bishop James C. Timlin, Bishop Stanislaus Brzana, Bishop DiLorenzo, and Bishop McCormick; Very Reverend and Reverend Fathers, Venerable Sisters of the various religious orders, Sisters and Brothers of the Polish National Catholic Church, the Roman Catholic Church, other churches and religious communities, Members of our local governments, Dear Friends. Ninety-five years ago a group of approximately 250 families gathered here and undertook a work which eventually led to the establishment of the Polish National Catholic Church. They gathered here in prayer and in solemn commitment to God that they sought to follow his Son Jesus Christ and to labor in his vineyard. Under the spiritual guidance of Father Francis Hodur who defied the wishes of his bishop, they sought to worship and work in the church which was their heritage, their Mother and guardian in the vicissitudes of their difficult life. The rest is history.

A division occurred in the Catholic Family in the United States of America. A division which caused many painful memories and which still remains among us.

In the report of our dialogue we write: "As bishops we are keenly aware that beyond our dialogue, the arduous spiritual task of the purification of memory is one in which all the people of our Churches must share, opening our hearts and minds to one another so that they are not encrusted with bitterness despite the pain all have felt." There is pain and hurt in our history which cannot be disguised. But we believe it is important for us to develop to the extent possible a common memory of this record, one that is serene, fair, sympathetic, just to all, and without imputation of motives.

We have made a significant journey along that path from the first steps which we mutually undertook in November of 1981.

We had invoked God the Holy Spirit to guide us in our dialogue and have committed it to the protection of the Blessed Virgin Mary, the Mother of Jesus Christ our Lord, the Mother of God.

Today marks a significant milestone in our journey to disperse bitterness and to assuage pain. May our prayer this afternoon contribute to the work and bear fruit for the unity of Christ's Kingdom.

Document 2

STATEMENT OF ROMAN CATHOLIC BISHOPS ENGAGED IN DIALOGUE WITH THE POLISH NATIONAL CATHOLIC BISHOPS

(Delivered at the Service of Healing, St. Stanislaus Polish National Catholic Cathedral, February 15, 1992. Statement approved October 16, 1990, at Stella Maris Retreat House, Skaneateles, New York. Permission to publish given by the Administrative Committee of the National Conference of Catholic Bishops, November 9, 1991)

A dispute arose in the Roman Catholic Church in the United States towards the end of the last century between some groups of Polish immigrants and Church authorities. The dispute was not over doctrine but over organizational matters.

On September 29, 1898, Bishop Michael J. Hoban of Scranton excommunicated the Reverend Francis Hodur, a priest of the Diocese of Scranton, because Father Hodur, without the permission of the Bishop, established a parish in Scranton, Pennsylvania. Thus, a decisive step was taken in a very complicated series of events which led to a break in Church unity, and to the founding of the Polish National Catholic Church with Francis Hodur as its first Bishop. It would be fair to say, we believe, that these actions led to consequences which, as far as we can judge today, went much further than their authors had intended or expected.

Feeling ran very deep in those days. Many still remember the great hurt and the anguish experienced as families split over the dispute and neighborhood friends virtually became enemies. It is difficult for us to appreciate how painful were the wounds on both sides during those tumultuous times.

It is understood that we should not attempt to rewrite history, nor should we judge the sincerity of the good people of those days. Neither can we pretend that these events were not what they were in that particularly troubled period of history. Those were difficult and trying days and no doubt the central figures in the dispute said and did what they thought to be just and proper under the circumstances.

But, we are confident that if Bishop Hoban and Bishop Hodur were alive today they would rejoice to see what has begun to happen in our time. Many of the issues which were fought over years ago are no longer in contention since the Second Vatican Council. Warm and loving relationships between our brothers and sisters of the Polish National Catholic Church and the Roman Catholic Church have begun to flower. Dialogue which was nonexistent for so long is now regular and productive.

As Roman Catholic Bishops engaged in this Dialogue with the Polish National Catholic Bishops, we want to reach out with the hand of friendship and Christian love to the clergy and faithful of the Polish National Catholic Church. We deeply regret all the times, that we, their brothers and sisters in the Lord, have been insensitive or have offended them in any way. We promise that we will do all in our power to see that those days never return.

In that same spirit which inspired Pope Paul VI and Patriarch Athenagoras to embrace on the Mount of Olives in 1964, we wish to *erase from the memory* and *consign to oblivion* the censure of excommunication which has been an obstacle to rapprochement in charity down to our own days.

We want to embrace the Bishops, Clergy, and Faithful of the Polish National Catholic Church. We hope and pray that we can put behind us all the polemics, disagreements, and misunderstandings of those by-gone days. We do, indeed, deplore the sad developments and mutual hostility which eventually led to the rupture of ecclesial communion.

We realize that this expression of our affection and good will cannot suffice to put an end to our differences. But, we are heartened and encouraged that with God's help and our mutual desire for healing and reconciliation, our Dialogue will lead us to live once again in full communion of faith, true concord, and sacramental life.

We call upon all to pray fervently for this intention. May the Lord Jesus lead and the Holy Spirit guide us to that visible union of faith which is the goal of all our efforts. May Mary, the Mother of God, intercede for us.

Document 3

STATEMENT OF POLISH NATIONAL CATHOLIC
BISHOPS ENGAGED IN DIALOGUE WITH THE
ROMAN CATHOLIC BISHOPS

*(Delivered at the Service of Healing, St. Stanislaus Polish
National Catholic Cathedral, February 15, 1992)*

We live in extraordinary times which have been marked with socio-political changes that have permitted peoples, once alienated and suspicious of one another, to now see each other in a more peaceful and fraternal light. The laborious struggles of diplomats and common people have given hope to the world.

Changes have also occurred in the religious world where the dawning of the ecumenical age is shining brightly in our time. Christians from every tradition are seriously working to know one another and respect one another's beliefs. Today the prayer of Jesus for unity among His disciples is given greater promise than ever.

It was on September 29, 1898 that the Bishop of Scranton, the Most Reverend Michael J. Hoban excommunicated the Reverend Francis Hodur, a priest of the Diocese of Scranton, for assuming the pastoral care of the congregation of Saint Stanislaus Church in Scranton, Pennsylvania without the bishop's consent.

Prior to this, Father Hodur and his people were determined to seek the help of the Holy Father in resolving the difficulties which arose in Scranton. On January 17, 1898 Father Hodur journeyed to Rome but his mission did not produce the results for which so many had hoped.

The birth of the Polish National Catholic Church was not due to matters of faith but rather over the administration of the temporalities of the church. This birth was especially painful, separating families and friends. Abuses were prevalent on both sides of the disputing parties. Painful as these abuses were, we recognize that each side acted in good faith and was convinced that it was doing God's will.

Today, the Polish National Catholic Church is primarily composed of believers who have been baptized and raised in this church. We do regret the pain and hurt which resulted from the actions which took place at the turn of the century. We sincerely pray to cast into oblivion the events of the past so that the names and actions of local churchmen and faithful, who acted in accordance with their conscience, be cleared of all allegations. We extend the hand of love, friendship and fraternity to our brothers and sisters of the Roman Catholic Church.

Since the inception of our dialogue in 1983, our churches have learned a great deal and discovered, as found in our common report, "Journeying Together in Christ," that there is more which unites us than divides us. In recent years, we have met in ecumenical forums both locally and internationally which have testified to our mutual desire for unity in Christ. The respect and fraternity which have been demonstrated in these encounters are signs of the Lord's presence in our midst.

Our journeying together has brought us to the current mile marker where we can mutually pray for a full sharing in a united ecclesiastical life and witness. We are unsure as to the times and means by which the Lord will lead us to this end. We are, however, strengthened by our common faith. This faith we share with the holy and just ones of every age who sought to do the Lord's will and among them Saint Paul the Apostle who encourages us in our ministry of reconciliation: "It was God who reconciled us to Himself through Christ and gave us the work of handing on this reconciliation ... so we are ambassadors for Christ; it is as though God were appealing through us, and the appeal that we make in Christ's name is: be reconciled to God." (2 Cor 5:18, 20)

May the glorious and ever Virgin Mary, Mother of God, and all the Saints intercede for us as we continue journeying together in Christ.

MOST REV. JOHN F. SWANTEK
Prime Bishop, Polish National Catholic Church

RT. REV. ANTHONY M. RYSZ
Chairman, PNCC Commission on Dialogue

Document 4

SPIRITUAL ADDRESS BY MOST REV. JOHN F. SWANTEK

*(Delivered at the Service of Healing, St. Stanislaus Polish
National Catholic Cathedral, February 15, 1992)*

Your Eminence, Cardinal Cassidy; my Brother Bishops, Very Rev. and Rev. Fathers, Rev. Sisters, and my Friends in Christ Jesus:

This is an historic day in the relationship of our two Catholic Churches. Since our dialogue began in 1983, the moment when both Churches responded to the Holy Spirit, representatives from the two Churches have met a number of times so that we could come to know each other better. For so many years in the past, it was a common practice for Christian bodies to emphasize their differences, but in this period of ecumenism, we have begun to discover that we hold many beliefs and practices in common: God the Father has created each and every one of us; God the Son, our Lord Jesus Christ, has redeemed us and taught us a way of life based on love, and it is incumbent on all Christians to follow this way; and God the Holy Spirit has sanctified us, causing us through His action to become children of God, members of Christ's Mystical Body, the Church, heirs to eternal life, and brothers and sisters to each other.

These Commandments of Love which Jesus taught were an almost insurmountable barrier for so many for so long, and yet all believed in good conscience that they were faithfully following Christ. We became plagued by the same problems as did the Apostles, who one day came to Jesus and said, "Teacher, we saw a man using your name to expel demons and we tried to stop him because he is not in our company." To this, Jesus responded, "Do not try to stop him. No man who performs a miracle in my name can at the same time speak ill of me. Anyone who is not against us is with us" (Mark 9:38-40). Even the chosen twelve did not know all who were followers of our Blessed Lord. How often have we acted as did the Apostles?

How often we failed to perceive the truths that we taught and their implications. In our respective Churches on Sundays and major feast days, we say the Nicene Creed which begins, "I believe in God, the Father, the Almighty, Maker of heaven and earth, of all that is seen and unseen." And yet it may not have occurred to many that we are acknowledging that God is our common Father, Who created all of us because He wanted us. God in Jesus was born on this earth to die for the sins of all, that all would have the opportunity to reach the Kingdom of God. Somehow we did not always admit that when we were baptized, we were baptized into Christ, became a member of His Body, the Church, and through the action of the Holy Spirit Who came to live in each and every one of us, we were united both to Jesus and to each other in God's family. How did we ever forget that every time we celebrate Mass, Christ Himself becomes present under the appearances of bread and wine, and through the receiving of the Holy Eucharist, we are truly joined to Christ, and through Him to each other, and this still happens today through Baptism and the Eucharist. Even though we are presently organically separated, we do share a unity through the Trinity.

In the Nicene Creed, we do confess our belief in the "one, holy, catholic and apostolic church." We acknowledge that the events of history have had a detrimental effect on Christ's Church and have actually impeded it from completely fulfilling the charge given to it by our Lord and Savior Jesus Christ. We cannot undo the shameful events of the past which were most likely executed by good people in good conscience, but not always with absolute fealty to the Gospel of our Lord Jesus Christ. But we must make a resolved effort, so that anything contrary to the mind of Christ is not repeated again.

It is very difficult to admit one's failings, for we all have a certain amount of pride as well as some blindness, but our Lord Jesus Christ is very much aware of how often we have failed Him, for we have acted in a sense at one time or another like Peter on the night that Christ was arrested. Through the things we said and did, we too denied that we knew Jesus.

The Holy Spirit has begun to move in the Churches. He has opened our eyes, so that we may see the state of the Church as God does — that we may see our discipleship as Jesus discerns it. The Holy Spirit has focused our attention on the will of God as it was proclaimed by Christ and recorded in the Holy Scriptures. Christ stated that He would establish a Church, and foreseeing what would happen because of human weakness and imperfection, our Lord knew that there would be problems, and the unity which existed prior to the Great Schism in 1054 would be fractured. In the Holy Scriptures, Jesus stated very emphatically, "So there shall be one flock, one Shepherd."

The ecumenical effort, caused by the Holy Spirit, is working to re-establish the unity which existed in the Church before the separation of East and West. This dialogue between two states of Christ's Church is working toward that goal which Christ has proclaimed and desires. When the late Prime Bishop Francis Rowinski invited Cardinal Krol to address our General Synod in 1986, he concluded his letter with these words, "May God the Holy Spirit guide us as we continue to work together for that unity for which our Lord prayed." That unity for which Christ prayed must be our goal.

When Cardinal Krol addressed the synod, he said, "Pope John XXIII's, of revered memory, repeated invitations to unity lacked any trace of a desire to absorb, to assimilate other churches and communities. He called for unity in essentials, not uniformity. He called for unity with diversity."

We have come here today to Saint Stanislaus Cathedral to express our love for Christ and for each other; to jointly admit that we failed to live the Gospel mandate of love; and in following the teaching of the Holy Scriptures in the example of Christ dying on the cross, we must mutually express forgiveness toward each other.

Ecumenism, I believe, is analogous to two people who are in love with each other and decide that they want to get married. They want to be married in church by Christ, making Him a part of this desired union. In that act of marriage, both individuals are willing to give up certain things in order to enter into a new life together, a life in which love, cooperation, and sacrifice are realities.

Jesus will forgive us as He forgave Peter, and He will ask us, "Do you love me more than these?" We should answer, "Yes, Lord; you know that I love you." He will then say, "Feed my lambs" (John 21:15).

We have begun "Journeying Together in Christ," which means that we are walking with Jesus as His disciples, following the way He taught, and we must make every effort not to stray from that path, because we must continue on the journey together in Christ, so that Jesus' wish, the type of unity that He wills, will one day be realized. This is expressed in the "Confession of Faith" which was written by Bishop Francis Hodur in 1913.

I believe in the need of uniting all followers of Christ's religion into one body of God's Church, and that the Church of Christ, Apostolic and Universal, is the representation of this Divine community of mankind, which the Savior proclaimed, for the realization of which all noble minded people labored, are still laboring, and for which the soul of man yearns, desiring truth, light, love, justice and consolation in God.

Document 5

LETTER OF HIS HOLINESS POPE JOHN PAUL II TO
MOST REV. JOHN SWANTEK

(February 4, 1992)

To Bishop John Swantek
Prime Bishop
Polish National Catholic Church

On the occasion of the visit to the headquarters of the Polish National Catholic Church by Cardinal Edward Cassidy, President of the Pontifical Council for Promoting Christian Unity, I send my personal greetings and prayers to you and to all your people.

With great interest I have learnt of the progress that has been made in your conversations with representatives of the Catholic Church. That dialogue has the purpose of overcoming the obstacles that prevent full communion between us. Through the dialogue and further steps taken recently, new hopes are raised that the events which some decades ago led to a break in the ecclesial unity which we had previously enjoyed can be put behind us, and that one day full communion in the one apostolic faith, sacramental life and mission, to which Christ calls us, can be restored.

I pray that we may imitate the fidelity of Mary, the Mother of God, and go forward together on the pilgrimage of faith towards the unity which is willed by the Lord and so much "desired by those who are attentively listening to what 'the Spirit is saying to the Churches' today (Rev 2:7, 11, 17)" (Encyclical Letter *Redemptoris Mater*, 30).

"Grace to you and peace from God our Father and the Lord Jesus Christ" (2 Cor 1:2).

From the Vatican, February 4, 1992
JOANNES PAULUS II

Document 6

'WITNESS TO RECONCILIATION'
BY CARDINAL EDWARD IDRIS CASSIDY

(Delivered at the Service of Healing, St. Stanislaus Polish National Catholic Cathedral, February 15, 1992)

Dear Friends:

This visit today to the city of Scranton is for me a major source of joy and encouragement. It is an honour to be present at, and in some ways be a partner in a ceremony which provides such hope for the future.

My visit has given me the occasion to meet with Bishop Timlin, who welcomed me personally on my arrival and who has been so helpful in arranging this meeting, and to greet the other Catholic bishops who have graced the occasion with their presence.

Of particular satisfaction to me has been the opportunity of having conversations with Bishop Swantek and the other bishops of the Polish National Catholic Church who have taken the trouble to come to Scranton in order to participate in this act of ecumenical witness.

The statements of the Bishops of the Polish National Catholic Church and the Roman Catholic Church in the United States of America, which are being made public during this ceremony, are acts of reconciliation and ecumenical commitment, resulting from the fruitful dialogue between the two Churches in this country.

While this is a significant step forward, the road to full communion still lies before us. But what has been accomplished is notable and can be interpreted as a willingness on the part of those involved to cooperate with the grace of God calling the followers of Christ to respond to the Saviour's priestly prayer for unity: **"that they may all be one . . . so that the world may believe . . ."** (John 17:21).

The Bishops of the Polish National Catholic Church and the Roman Catholic Church have not written a common declaration. But they have written parallel statements embodying similar themes, revealing in many ways their oneness of mind and heart.

There are a number of important themes in the statements and I would like to mention five of them.

First, both statements express the desire for unity:

> "Our journeying together has brought us to the current mile marker where we can mutually pray for a full sharing in a united ecclesiastical life and witness." (Polish National Catholic Bishops).

> ". . . We are heartened and encouraged that with God's help and our mutual desire for healing and reconciliation, our dialogue will lead us to live once again [in full] communion of faith, true concord, and sacramental life." (Roman Catholic Bishops).

Secondly, both statements express the desire to heal memories. Very often the bitter memories of harsh encounters in the past linger in such a way as to make reconciliation difficult. Both invite their communities into a process of the healing of bitter memories. Thus the Polish National Catholic Bishops say:

"We do regret the pain and hurt which resulted from the actions which took place at the turn of the century. We sincerely pray to cast into oblivion the events of the past so that the names and actions of local churchmen and faithful, who acted in accordance with their conscience, be cleared of all allegations."

And, the Roman Catholic Bishops recall the spirit in which Pope Paul VI and Patriarch Athenagoras of Constantinople embraced each other on the Mount of Olives in 1964, which led the following year to a joint declaration in which they consigned to the past centuries of bitter memories and called for a dialogue to lead the Catholic and Orthodox Churches to live once again in full communion. They state that:

"We should not judge the sincerity of the good people of those days. . . . No doubt the central figures in the dispute said and did what they thought to be just and proper under the circumstances."

"We wish to 'erase from the memory' and consign to oblivion the censure of excommunication which has been an obstacle to rapprochement in charity down to our own days."

Thirdly, through these statements each offers the hand of friendship to the other, as the confirmation of a new relationship. Thus regretting the pain and hurt which resulted from actions at the turn of the century, the Bishops of the Polish National Catholic Church "extend the hand of love, friendship and fraternity to our brothers and sisters of the Roman Catholic Church."

And, expressing regret for the times they have been insensitive or offensive toward their partner, and promising that "those days never return," the Roman Catholic Bishops indicate that they "want to reach out with the hand of friendship and Christian love to the clergy and faithful of the Polish National Catholic Church."

Fourthly, and very significantly for the possibilities of achieving full communion, both state that issues of faith were not among the events leading to separation: "the birth of the Polish National Catholic Church was not due to matters of faith but rather over the administration of the temporalities of the Church" (PNCC). "This dispute was not over doctrine, but over organizational matters" (RCC).

To be able to say that matters of faith were not involved in the original dispute makes a momentous difference in the efforts to achieve unity. In some of our dialogues where disputes about faith were involved when divisions occurred centuries ago, it is difficult to overcome some of these differences. How fortunate it is that you can engage in a process of ecumenical healing free of the burden of having to resolve serious differences in faith. This however makes efforts to achieve full communion even more urgent. For separation by its very nature creates a culture which always seeks to build on separation itself no matter what the original reasons for division were.

During the recent Special Assembly for Europe of the Synod of Bishops, November 28-December 14, 1991, Fraternal Delegates from Orthodox, Anglican and Protestant churches of Europe were invited to take part. The Fraternal Delegate representing the Church of England, Bishop Mark Santer, during his address to the Synod made an important comment on the dynamics of division and what they produce. His words are worth recalling here. He said:

"The most serious obstacle to the restoration of communion between divided Christians is ... the breach of communion itself. I do not wish to appear less than serious about the doctrinal issues which lie between us, but I will nevertheless say with some confidence that few of those issues would actually justify a breach of communion if we were not divided already. But once communion is broken, communities tend to drift further apart. They no longer acknowledge a common authority, and divergencies of law, of administration and mentality naturally develop.... Once separated, ecclesial communities develop different cultures which are extraordinarily difficult to reconcile — in, for instance, spirituality, and in the way authority is exercised, and in the way the Christian community related to the secular world."

I believe there is much truth in Bishop Santer's words. But here, through dialogue and renewed contacts in recent years and today, with these statements of reconciliation, the Polish National Catholic Church and the Roman Catholic Church are taking serious steps to replace division, and the culture it produces, with a process of reconciliation. How urgent it is that this continue. And since neither side sees disputes in faith at the origin of their separation, how much more opportunity that seems to give for reconciliation.

Fifthly, it is important that both statements end with an expression of our common heritage. Namely in seeking to do the will of Christ, both call upon Mary, the Mother of God, to intercede for us as we continue "journeying together in Christ," "to that visible union of faith which is the goal of all our efforts."

Unity, then, is urgent because the Lord himself wills that his disciples be one, that they be free of the scandal of division, "so that the world may believe." Unity is urgent also for the sake of our people. Pope John Paul II has spoken often of unity as a pastoral priority because disunity affects our people in their everyday Christian lives. We see this especially when disunity keeps us from coming together for the eucharist, and in the challenges of a mixed marriage. But we see this in other ways as well.

I want to express my personal appreciation for the important step you have taken today, in the renewed commitment toward reconciliation expressed in these statements and to which we are all witnesses. To cite St. Paul's words in the letter to the Philippians:

"I am sure that he who began a good work in you will bring it to completion at the day of Jesus Christ." (Phil. 1:6).

Thank you again for the warmth of your hospitality towards me today. Be assured of my prayers for the continued success of this important dialogue between the Polish National Catholic Church and the National Conference of Catholic Bishops.

Document 7

His Eminence, Edward Cardinal Cassidy, President of the Pontifical Council for Promoting Christian Unity, has informed Archbishop William H. Keeler, President of the National Conference of Catholic Bishops (NCCB), that members of the Polish National Catholic Church in the United States and Canada (PNCC) may receive the Sacraments of Penance, Holy Communion and Anointing of the Sick from Roman Catholic priests if they ask for them on their own, are properly disposed and not otherwise excluded from the sacraments.

The Cardinal's letter is an answer to a request from the National Clergy Conference of the PNCC expressing hope for increased sacramental possibilities between the Churches as they moved toward unity. Prime Bishop John Swantek of the PNCC forwarded this expression of hope to His Holiness Pope John Paul II a little over two years ago. Archbishop Daniel Pilarczyk, then President of the NCCB, also made a formal request that the PNCC be considered in the same condition as the Oriental Churches (e.g., Eastern Orthodox) as far as these sacraments are concerned. Roman Catholic Canon Law specifies this is a matter for the judgment of the Holy See in Canon 844 which states:

Can. 844 — §1. Catholic ministers may licitly administer the sacraments to Catholic members of the Christian faithful only and, likewise, the latter may licitly receive the sacraments only from Catholic ministers with due regard for §§2, 3, and 4 of this canon, and can. 861, §2.

§2. Whenever necessity requires or genuine spiritual advantage suggests, and provided that the danger of error or indifferentism is avoided, it is lawful for the faithful for whom it is physically or morally impossible to approach a Catholic minister, to receive the sacraments of penance, Eucharist, and anointing of the sick from non-Catholic ministers in whose churches these sacraments are valid.

§3. Catholic ministers may licitly administer the sacraments of penance, Eucharist and anointing of the sick to members of the oriental churches which do not have full communion with the Catholic Church, if they ask on their own for the sacraments and are properly disposed. This holds also for members of other churches, which in the judgment of the Apostolic See are in the same condition as the oriental churches as far as these sacraments are concerned.

§4. If the danger of death is present or other grave necessity, in the judgment of the diocesan bishop or the conference of bishops, Catholic ministers may licitly administer these sacraments to other Christians who do not have full communion with the Catholic Church, who cannot approach a minister of their own community and on their own ask for it, provided they manifest Catholic faith in these sacraments and are properly disposed.

§5. For the cases in §§2, 3, and 4, neither the diocesan bishop nor the conference of bishops is to enact general norms except after consultation with at least the local competent authority of the interested non-Catholic church or community.

This is indeed an important development in the on-going dialogue taking place between the PNCC and the RC Churches. It means that Polish National Catholics may receive these three sacraments in the Roman Catholic Church under the same conditions as Roman Catholics if they ask for them on their own.

Now that a favorable response has been received from the Vatican, practical pastoral instructions and guidelines on how this is to be best implemented will be forthcoming in the near future.

All the bishops of the dialogue welcome this judgment by the Holy See and ask the priests and faithful of both Churches to accept it as one positive step forward toward the realization of Our Lord's prayer that as His followers we may be one as He and the Father are one. More is to be accomplished and the "Journey Together in Christ" is not yet at an end. The bishops ask the support of the prayers of all the faithful that with the Lord's help, with the grace of the Holy Spirit, and with the intercession of Mary we may be brought to its needed and much-longed-for goal, full unity.

In its recent sessions (Buffalo, June 1992; Boston, October 1992) the Bishops' Dialogue has investigated the role of the Bishop of Rome as successor of St. Peter and promoter of unity. The meeting in Dearborn Heights, Michigan on April 22, 1993 explored the understanding of ecclesiastical communion as the form of unity specific to the Church and various models of unity to express unity in an appropriate and adequate way.

Both Roman Catholics and Polish National Catholics should rejoice and be grateful that we have come to this day. It should spur us on to even greater efforts to resolve whatever obstacles to full communion still remain.

Document 8

RESPONSE TO THE VATICAN ANNOUNCEMENT ON
SACRAMENTAL SHARING BY THE POLISH NATIONAL
CATHOLIC CHURCH BISHOPS
WHO ARE PART OF THE DIALOGUE

(April 22, 1993)

We welcome with joy the announcement from the Vatican concerning the status of the Polish National Catholic Church in regards to Canon 844. This positive announcement, the result of dialogue, inspires hope in our "Journeying Together in Christ."

The clarification regarding the opportunity to receive the sacraments of Penance, Eucharist and Anointing of the Sick, under certain conditions strengthens those fraternal ties which already exist. We trust that, under the guidance of the Holy Spirit, we may collaborate on developing guidelines which will increase our opportunities for pastoral care and a common witness.

The dialogue will continue between our two Churches as we work to realize that unity for which our Lord Jesus Christ prayed.

PNCC DIALOGUE COMMISSION
April 22, 1993
Dearborn Heights, Michigan

Document 9

PASTORAL GUIDELINES CONCERNING ADMISSION OF POLISH NATIONAL CATHOLICS TO SACRAMENTS IN THE ROMAN CATHOLIC CHURCH

(Promulgated in a March 13, 1996, letter to the Bishops of the United States from Most Rev. Oscar H. Lipscomb)

For some years there has been a cordial dialogue taking place between bishops of the Polish National Catholic Church and the Roman Catholic Church. This dialogue seeks the healing of a division which occurred within the American Catholic community in this century, and the recovery of its unity. In that context the question arose whether there would be occasions on which Polish National Catholics might be admitted to sacraments celebrated in the Roman Catholic Church.

It is the understanding of the Roman Catholic Church that the celebration of sacraments is an action of the celebrating community made within the community itself in which the celebration signifies oneness of faith, worship and life. Accordingly, participation in the sacraments is normally restricted to those who are members of the community. However, certain exceptions can occur.

Thus, for example, the Roman Catholic Code of Canon Law (Canon 844.3) reads: *"Catholic ministers may licitly administer the sacraments of penance, Eucharist and anointing of the sick to members of oriental churches who do not have full communion with the Catholic Church, if they ask on their own for the sacraments and are properly disposed. This holds also for members of other churches, which in the judgement of the Apostolic See are in the same condition as the oriental churches as far as these sacraments are concerned."*

In the course of the Polish National Catholic-Roman Catholic dialogue, "it seemed clear to the Roman Catholic participants on the basis of the evidence that the bishops of the Polish National Catholic Church are validly ordained bishops in apostolic succession." In light of this the National Conference of Catholic Bishops inquired whether in the judgment of the Apostolic See the canon cited would apply to the Polish National Catholic Church. In due course, Cardinal Edward I. Cassidy, president of the Pontifical Council for Promoting Christian Unity, sent a reply in behalf of the Holy See, saying "there are sufficient reasons to respond affirmatively to the request."

Application of Canon 844.3 to Polish National Catholics

Certain specifications should be observed. First of all, this clarification responds only to the question posed concerning the Polish National Catholic Church in the United States and Canada. It does not address the status of any other church. Thus, for example, the Polish Catholic Church in Poland, which sprang from the Polish National Catholic Church and is now autonomous, is not included in this response of the Holy See, nor are the other churches of the Union of Utrecht. The specific pastoral context in which the question was raised concerned the fact that members of the Polish National Catholic Church sometimes found themselves in situations in which they did not have access to the sacramental ministration of their own priests. This pastoral consideration was the framework and the primary motive around which the response of the Holy See was made.

The decision applies to members in good standing of the Polish National Catholic Church who are not otherwise individually impeded by canonical sanctions of the Roman Catholic Church. This restriction would apply to those individuals who once were Roman Catholics and incurred a sanction which has not subsequently been lifted by the Roman Catholic Church. Such, for instance, would be the case of a Roman Catholic priest who set aside his priestly obligations without a dispensation. Others might be impeded from receiving the Eucharist because of their marital situation.

Roman Catholic sacramental ministers should all be advised by their pastors of this decision of the Holy See so they are prepared to apply it consistently and generously when the sacraments of Holy Communion, penance, and anointing of the sick are requested of them by Polish National Catholics. Consistency of practice is very important in this matter, not only in centers where Polish National Catholics are numerous, but also in areas removed from such centers where Polish National Catholics, not having ready access to their own bishops and priests, may approach Roman Catholic priests with requests for the sacraments.

Sacramental ministers of the Roman Catholic Church may admit Polish National Catholics to the sacraments of penance, the Eucharist, and anointing of the sick, when they ask and are properly disposed to approach the sacraments with faith, repentance, and a firm purpose of amendment (conditions which all Christians must fulfill in approaching the sacraments). No additional restrictions apply. The additional restrictions which do apply to Protestants (such as serious need of the sacraments and the inability to receive them from their own ministers, cf. Canon 844.4) do not apply in these cases. It can safely be presumed that Polish National Catholics hold a faith in these three sacraments in harmony with the faith held by Roman Catholics, and ought not be questioned on this.

While the law of the Roman Catholic Church (Canon 844.3) makes generous provisions, it should still be kept in mind that these cases are seen as exceptional, not as the norm. Normally Polish National Catholics, it is expected, will seek the sacraments from their own bishops and priests, and only on certain occasions approach Roman Catholic sacramental ministers.

Since full communion between our churches has not yet been achieved, in no instance is a Roman Catholic priest permitted to concelebrate the Eucharist with Polish National Catholic priests (Canon 908).

Application of Canon 844.2 to Roman Catholics

Nothing is changed with respect to Roman Catholics seeking admission to the sacraments from priests of the Polish National Catholic Church, and the response from the Holy See did not touch that issue. According to Canon 844.2, Roman Catholics may approach the sacramental ministers of other churches only when four conditions are met:

1. when this is required by necessity or suggested by way of true spiritual advantage — a condition that might be met in a number of cases,
2. the danger of error or indifferentism is avoided — a condition that might readily be met in most cases,
3. it is virtually impossible (either physically or morally impossible) for Roman Catholics to receive these sacraments from their own minister — a condition that might be the least likely to be fulfilled since Roman Catholic

ministers of the sacraments are generally present in neighborhoods where their Polish National Catholic counterparts are found, and

4. they seek them only of a church whose sacraments are valid — a condition which in the case of the Polish National Catholic Church is fulfilled.

Thus, the requirements differ somewhat. Out of respect for individual consciences and sensitivity to individual spiritual needs, cases should be responded to on an individual basis. General public invitations to communicate are not appropriate.

Different Customs

In this matter all should know about and respect the different customs of our churches. Polish National Catholics generally receive Communion on the tongue by intinction. They receive either kneeling or standing. Roman Catholics usually receive the Sacred Host standing. They receive either in the hand or on the tongue, as the communicant wishes. Communion is not distributed under both kinds at all Roman Catholic Masses. When it is, after receiving the Host, the communicant proceeds to a second Eucharistic minister who offers the chalice containing the Precious Blood. Roman Catholics have the option not to receive under both kinds. In the administration of Holy Communion in the Roman Catholic Church, bishops, priests, and deacons are also assisted by lay ministers of the Eucharist, both men and women. This is not the case in the Polish National Catholic Church. The eucharistic fast before receiving Holy Communion is two hours in the Polish National Catholic Church, one hour in the Roman Catholic Church.

Regrettably our churches are still divided. But we do hope that the clarification we have received from Rome will advance our churches toward that full communion of faith and life that is both Christ's promise and His will for us. At the same time we trust it will be a source of pastoral and sacramental support for our people as they live out their faith.

Document 10

PASTORAL LETTER BY MOST REV. JAMES C. TIMLIN

*(Delivered at the Polish National Catholic Church's
One Hundredth Anniversary Mass, St. Stanislaus Polish
National Catholic Cathedral, March 9, 1997)*

*To the esteemed Bishops, Priests, and all our cherished Brothers and
Sisters of the Polish National Catholic Church on the occasion of the
One Hundredth Anniversary of the Founding of the
Polish National Catholic Church*

Dearly Beloved in Christ:

On countless occasions both as a priest and bishop, I have
been touched deeply as I stood before God's altar and watched the
father of the bride accompany his precious daughter to the place
and moment of her marriage. Most of the time, tears and smiles
alternated with each other on the father's countenance: joy for her
joy, sorrow for his separation from her. And, in between, flickers
of hope: "She will have her own family, I will be a grandfather, and
differently but somehow she will be home again."

It is with that confusion of feeling that I embrace all of you
on this occasion of the one hundredth anniversary of the founding of the Polish National Catholic Church, your marriage to a
century.

My joy today is for your joy over the splendid accomplish-
ments of one hundred years of struggle, growth, pain, endurance,
success, increase, advance, hope, and courage. I pray for you and
with you that God's choicest blessings, deepest consolations, and

unparalleled rewards may come to all those who have given themselves so generously to build God's kingdom on earth in your outstanding community of faith. I greet you one and all in the peace of Christ and assure you of my heartfelt goodwill as you set out on our common pilgrimage of faith into the second century of your Church's life.

How disingenuous of me it would be to so openly relate the genuine joy I feel with you and for you, and at the same time hide my sorrow as the Bishop of Scranton, the diocese wherein your suffering was experienced to the point of causing a breaking away, a separation, a rupture, the pain of which we all feel to this very day.

Truly beloved, that both sides were to blame, that either side was to blame, or that one side was to blame more than the other, none of these assessments of the past console me or lessen my sorrow. In fact, they only remind me of the tragically sad day in the history of the Diocese of Scranton when the world was given reason to believe that the Heavenly Father did not send Jesus, because the prayer of Jesus went unanswered: ". . . that all may be one as you, Father, are in me, and I in you; . . . that the world may believe that you sent me" (Jn. 17:21).

My Brothers and Sisters, it is your hundredth anniversary. And I, your Brother James, Bishop of Scranton, believe the moment has arrived to take Saint Paul at his word, a word I speak both to the Roman Catholic Church and the Polish National Catholic Church, and the word is this: ". . . now in Christ Jesus you who were once far off have been brought near through the blood of Christ. It is he who is our peace and who made the two of us one by breaking down the barrier of hostility that kept us apart" (Eph. 2:13-14).

With that barrier removed, I come to you, and with profound sorrow I beg your forgiveness for every offense, misunderstanding, unkind act, mistaken judgment, or any other thought, word, or deed ever committed against you through prejudice, thoughtlessness, or suspicious misgivings on the part of anyone in the Roman Catholic community. And I pledge on the occasion of this meaningful anniversary that my desire, as long as I live, will be to ever strive to restore the unity that was once ours so that our nearness purchased by the blood of Christ will be all he intended it to be.

The father of the bride, whom I mentioned at the start, feels flickers of hope as he thinks of the days ahead and the pleasures of the extended family. I must part company with him on that score for my hope is indeed overwhelming as I view our future.

Our communities, the Polish National Catholic Church and the Roman Catholic Church, are truly exceptional, in that almost constant advance has characterized what our Churches have been accomplishing. Other ecclesial efforts to come together have not been as fortunate, despite the best of intentions and efforts.

Rejoice and hope with me as I announce to you signs of God's love and grace descending upon us. I note but three.

First, through fraternal sharing in study and close, warm friendship, Polish National Catholic and Roman Catholic Bishops and clergy have embraced one another in Christ Jesus with a love and consideration literally unthinkable just a few years ago. The depth of honesty and concern between us has led to a dialogue which has enabled us to experience not just an exchange of ideas but, in the words of our Holy Father, Pope John Paul II, "an exchange of gifts." We Roman Catholics have been enriched many times over through sharing with your hierarchy and clergy. And I know, because of their loving manifestations, they have also. Never do we gather without being touched by God so that ever-new possibilities for coming together open before us.

Second, even though we cannot forget the past, which in a sense we have laid to rest, we can recognize the beautiful and blinding light of God's mercy on us all in our ability under certain circumstances to share sacramentally. The Holy Eucharist, Christ's gift of total, unconditional love, given to empower us to love, is our common gift. That sacramental presence of Jesus, the very power of God which gives to each of our communities our very identity as a Church, can now draw us together. May the good God be praised forever because he has lifted us up to such heights.

Third and lastly, but, practically speaking, of supreme importance, our dear people are opening themselves to the healing grace of Christ Our Savior. Going, and in many instances gone, is that paralyzing fear which made us believe that listening and loving our distant brothers and sisters would somehow betray our own community. That fear is and has been replaced by the wisdom of the cross: the more we die to all selfishness, the more we live in God, our only true life. The more we love and draw near to those from whom we have strayed, the greater is our unity with those with whom we stand.

For these reasons and many more, my dear Brothers and Sisters, you must be able to see that my hope is no flicker but a blazing fire, obviously lit and sustained by God, by God most merciful.

I bring my most loving sentiments toward you to a close by asking you to reflect deeply on an instance in Our Lord's life which my dear brother, Bishop Swantek, mentioned during his homily in St. Peter's Cathedral on January 23 of this year.

The event is mentioned in St. Mark's Gospel (9:38-40):

> John said to him, "Teacher, we saw a man using your name to expel demons and we tried to stop him because he is not of our company." Jesus said in reply: "Do not try to stop him. No man who performs a miracle using my name can at the same time speak ill of me. Anyone who is not against us is with us."

I ask you to keep this exquisite instance in mind as we continue our joyful journey. It comes straight from the heart of our Savior through the gracious mind and heart of your Prime Bishop.

And, what does it say? Simply this: Roman Catholics and Polish National Catholics, open your eyes. Behold the wonderful works of God accomplished in one another. Never stop gazing at them in love and admiration. And then you will see the bond that unites you, and you will thankfully embrace one another, and God will be thrice blessed and glorified because his Son's heart will have truly entered ours.

O my Brothers and Sisters, what an opportunity is ours to enable all around us to know again that the Father has sent Jesus to us because that same world sees our oneness — again, in the words of Jesus: ". . . that all may be one . . . that the world may believe that you sent me" (Jn. 17:21).

Isaiah delights our hearts as he describes the object of our well-founded hope for our unity: "Then your light shall break forth like the dawn, and your wound shall be quickly healed; . . . then you shall call, and the Lord will answer, you shall call for help, and he will say: Here I am!" (Is. 58:8-9).

That, my dear Brothers and Sisters, is what I hear and feel because of your warm kindness in having me here with you today to celebrate your anniversary: God himself embracing, loving, reassuring all of us and whispering gently to each, "Here I am!"

Sincerely yours in Christ,

MOST REVEREND JAMES C. TIMLIN, D.D.
Bishop of Scranton

Document 11

*(Accepted at the Twentieth General Synod of the Polish
National Catholic Church, Chicago, Illinois, October 6,
1998, after prior approval by the PNCC Doctrine
Commission, September 2, 1997, and the PNCC Bishops
Conference, September 3, 1997)*

1. *Preamble*

A. In principle, all Polish National Catholics are obliged to
receive the sacraments, including Holy Eucharist, only from
ministers of the Polish National Catholic Church (PNCC).
In this way, Polish National Catholics demonstrate their unity
both with the Lord and with each other. The PNCC believes
that the legitimate reception of this sacrament requires a prior
unity of faith in the reality and meaning of the Eucharist.
Because this unity does not yet exist among all churches, the
PNCC does not ordinarily authorize the reception of the
Eucharist by Polish National Catholics from non-PNCC
ministers.

B. At the same time, the PNCC recognizes that, due to their
conditions of life, not all Polish National Catholics are able to
receive the sacraments from Polish National Catholic ministers on a regular basis. Members of the PNCC who live or

travel far from Polish National Catholic parishes fall into this category, as do students living away from home. For this reason and as a result of the progress achieved in ecumenical dialogue between the Polish National Catholic and Roman Catholic Churches, the PNCC requested the Roman Catholic Church to admit such Polish National Catholics to the sacraments of Eucharist, Penance, and Holy Unction. Following a favorable response by the Holy See, the American Roman Catholic bishops adopted and published a document entitled *Pastoral Guidelines Concerning Admission of Polish National Catholics to Sacraments in the Roman Catholic Church (Canon 844)*.

C. The present document represents the PNCC's response to this action by the Roman Catholic Church and sets forth guidelines for Polish National Catholics who desire to receive sacraments from Roman Catholic ministers, as well as terms under which Roman Catholics may be admitted to sacraments in the PNCC.

2. *Reception of Sacraments by Polish National Catholics from Roman Catholic Ministers*

A. Polish National Catholics who are unable to receive the sacraments of Eucharist, Penance, or Holy Unction within the PNCC are authorized to receive these sacraments from Roman Catholic ministers. The same prerequisites for the reception of these sacraments within the PNCC also apply to such reception within the Roman Catholic Church — above all, in the case of the Eucharist, the absence of grave (mortal) sin and observance of a two-hour eucharistic fast.

B. Polish National Catholics should be aware that the discipline governing the administration of these sacraments in the Roman Catholic Church differs from that of the PNCC. For example, Roman Catholic clergy variously administer the Eucharist under the species of bread alone in the hand or on the tongue, of bread and wine separately, or by intinction. Polish National Catholics should receive the Eucharist under the species of bread (or bread and wine by intinction) on the tongue. Moreover, in the Roman Catholic Church, auricular (private) confession is the norm for the reception of the Sacrament of Penance (Reconciliation), and Polish National Catholics seeking this sacrament from a Roman Catholic minister ordinarily will make their confession in this manner.

C. There may arise special occasions, apart from cases of necessity, when it would be appropriate for Polish National Catholics to receive the Eucharist from Roman Catholic ministers (e.g., weddings, funerals). Such reception is authorized by the PNCC.

D. Under no circumstances are Eucharistic concelebrations by Polish National Catholic and Roman Catholic clergy authorized, for such concelebrations would indicate a oneness of faith and order that does not yet exist between the two Churches.

3. *Reception of the Sacraments by Roman Catholics in the PNCC*

A. The Polish National Catholic Church does not object to the reception by Roman Catholics of the sacraments of Eucharist, Penance, and Holy Anointing from Polish

National Catholic ministers. Polish National Catholic clergy should do nothing to impede such reception. At the same time, they should not issue general invitations for Roman Catholics to receive the Eucharist in the PNCC.

B. In all such cases, however, Roman Catholics are urged to respect the discipline of their own church as set forth in the American Roman Catholic bishops' *Pastoral Guidelines* and applicable canonical legislation.

4. These guidelines come into effect upon publication and remain in force until such time as they are formally revised or abrogated.

Appendix II

Polish National Catholic-Roman Catholic Dialogue: Sessions, Participants, and Topics of Discussion, 1989-2002

(Note: The first nine meetings of the PNCC-RC Dialogue, from its inception in 1984 until 1989, are compiled in the book Journeying Together in Christ.*)*

MEETING #10

June 1-2, 1989 — Washington Retreat House
(Washington, D.C.)
Hosted by the Roman Catholic Church

PNCC	RCC
Rt. Rev. Anthony M. Rysz	Most Rev. Stanislaus Brzana
Rt. Rev. Joseph I. Nieminski	Most Rev. James C. Timlin
Very Rev. Stanley Skrzypek	Most Rev. Alfred Abramowicz
Very Rev. Sigmund Peplowski	Rev. Msgr. John Gallagher
Rev. A. Waine Kargul	Rev. John Hotchkin
Dr. Joseph Wieczerzak	

Topics of Discussion
1. The Polish National Catholic Church: Its Roman Catholic Origins
2. A Brief History of the Polish National Catholic Church and Its Origins
3. Excommunication of Bishop Hodur

MEETING #11

November 28-29, 1989 — Residence of Archbishop William H. Keeler (Baltimore, Md.)
Hosted by the Roman Catholic Archdiocese of Baltimore

PNCC	RCC
Rt. Rev. Anthony M. Rysz	Most Rev. Stanislaus Brzana
Rt. Rev. Joseph I. Nieminski	Most Rev. James C. Timlin
Very Rev. Stanley Skrzypek	Most Rev. Alfred Abramowicz
Rev. A. Waine Kargul	Rev. John Hotchkin
	Rev. Joseph F. Mytych

Topics of Discussion
1. *Journeying Together in Christ*
2. Collegiality of Roman Catholic Bishops with the Pope
3. Collegiality of Polish National Catholic Bishops with the Bishops of the Old Catholic Union of Utrecht
4. Excommunication of Bishop Hodur

MEETING #12

May 2-3, 1990 — St. Stanislaus Cathedral (Scranton, Pa.)
Hosted by the Polish National Catholic Church

PNCC	RCC
Rt. Rev. Anthony M. Rysz	Most Rev. Stanislaus Brzana
Rt. Rev. Joseph I. Nieminski	Most Rev. James C. Timlin
Very Rev. Stanley Skrzypek	Most Rev. Alfred Abramowicz
Rev. A. Waine Kargul	Rev. John Hotchkin
	Rev. Joseph F. Mytych

Topics of Discussion
1. *Journeying Together in Christ*
2. Union of Utrecht
3. Sacramental Sharing
4. History of Old Catholic–Roman Catholic Relations
5. Excommunication of Bishop Hodur by Bishop Hoban

MEETING #13

October 15–16, 1990 — Stella Maris Retreat House
(Syracuse, N.Y.)
Hosted by the Roman Catholic Diocese of Ogdensburg

PNCC	RCC
Rt. Rev. Anthony M. Rysz	Most Rev. Stanislaus Brzana
Rt. Rev. Joseph I. Nieminski	Most Rev. James C. Timlin
Very Rev. Stanley Skrzypek	Most Rev. Alfred Abramowicz
	Rev. John Hotchkin
	Rev. Joseph F. Mytych

Topics of Discussion
1. Canon 844.3
2. Old Catholic–Roman Catholic Relations
3. Primacy in the Church
4. Excommunication of Bishop Hodur by Bishop Hoban

MEETING #14

May 22-23, 1991 — Queen of Apostles Renewal Center
(Mississauga, Ont., Canada)
Hosted by the Roman Catholic Church

PNCC	RCC
Rt. Rev. Anthony M. Rysz	Most Rev. Stanislaus Brzana
Rt. Rev. Joseph I. Nieminski	Most Rev. James C. Timlin
Very Rev. Stanley Skrzypek	Most Rev. Alfred Abramowicz
Rev. A. Waine Kargul	Rev. Joseph F. Mytych

Topics of Discussion
1. Canon 844.3
2. The Jurisdiction and Primacy of the Pope
3. Jurisdiction of Bishops of the PNCC
4. PNCC Constitution
5. Responsible Parenthood

MEETING #15

November 6-7, 1991 — Diocesan Chancery (Scranton, Pa.)
Hosted by the Roman Catholic Diocese of Scranton

PNCC	RCC
Rt. Rev. Anthony M. Rysz	Most Rev. Stanislaus Brzana
Rt. Rev. Thaddeus S. Peplowski	Most Rev. James C. Timlin
Very Rev. Joseph Tomczyk	Most Rev. Alfred Abramowicz
Very Rev. Stanley Skrzypek	Rev. John Hotchkin
Very Rev. Sigmund Peplowski	Rev. Joseph F. Mytych

Topics of Discussion
1. Principle of Collegiality as Understood in the Roman Catholic Church
2. Collegiality in the Church
3. Visit of Cardinal Cassidy
4. International Bishops' Conference
5. The Papacy and the Council

MEETING #16

*June 3–4, 1992 — Holy Mother of the Rosary Cathedral
(Buffalo, N.Y.)
Hosted by the Polish National Catholic Church*

PNCC	RCC
Rt. Rev. Anthony M. Rysz	Most Rev. Stanislaus Brzana
Rt. Rev. Thaddeus S. Peplowski	Most Rev. James C. Timlin
Very Rev. Joseph Tomczyk	Most Rev. Alfred Abramowicz
Very Rev. Stanley Skrzypek	Most Rev. Edward Head
Very Rev. Sigmund Peplowski	Most Rev. Edward Grosz
Rev. A. Waine Kargul	Rev. John Hotchkin
	Rev. Joseph F. Mytych
	Rev. Francis Mazur
	Rev. Bonaventure F. Hayes, O.F.M.

Topics of Discussion
1. The Authority Given by Jesus to Peter and All the Apostles
2. Episcopacy and Collegiality in the Polish National Catholic Church

3. Canon 844.3
4. Service of Healing — Scranton, Pa.
5. Buffalo Covenant
6. Pastoral Guidelines

MEETING #17

*October 28-29, 1992 — Pastoral Institute of the
Archdiocese of Boston (Mass.)
Hosted by the Roman Catholic Archdiocese of Boston*

PNCC	RCC
Rt. Rev. Anthony M. Rysz	Most Rev. Stanislaus Brzana
Rt. Rev. Thaddeus S. Peplowski	Most Rev. James C. Timlin
Very Rev. Joseph Tomczyk	Most Rev. Alfred Abramowicz
Very Rev. Stanley Skrzypek	Rev. John Hotchkin
Very Rev. Sigmund Peplowski	Rev. Joseph F. Mytych
Rev. A. Waine Kargul	Rev. Edward M. O'Flaherty, S.J.
	Rev. Brian Daley, S.J.

Topics of Discussion
1. Canon 844.3
2. Union of Utrecht
3. Examination of Lay and Clerical Feelings Regarding Full Communion
4. The Bishop of Rome as the Successor of Peter

MEETING #18

April 21-22, 1993 — Our Savior Parish
(Dearborn Heights, Mich.)
Hosted by the Polish National Catholic Church

PNCC	RCC
Rt. Rev. Anthony M. Rysz	Most Rev. Stanislaus Brzana
Rt. Rev. Thaddeus S. Peplowski	Most Rev. James C. Timlin
Very Rev. Joseph Tomczyk	Most Rev. Alfred Abramowicz
Very Rev. Sigmund Peplowski	Rev. Msgr. Leonard P. Blair
Rev. A. Waine Kargul	Rev. John Hotchkin
	Rev. Joseph F. Mytych

Topics of Discussion
1. Canon 844.3
2. The Papacy in Light of the Church as Communion
3. Models for Unity

MEETING #19

October 27-28, 1993 — Motherhouse of the Daughters of
Mary of the Immaculate Conception (Hartford, Conn.)
Hosted by the Roman Catholic Diocese of Hartford

PNCC	RCC
Rt. Rev. Anthony M. Rysz	Most Rev. Stanislaus Brzana
Rt. Rev. Thaddeus S. Peplowski	Most Rev. James C. Timlin
Rt. Rev. Joseph Tomczyk	Most Rev. Alfred Abramowicz
Very Rev. Stanley Skrzypek	Rev. John Hotchkin
Very Rev. Sigmund Peplowski	Rev. Joseph F. Mytych
Rev. A. Waine Kargul	

Topics of Discussion
1. Models of Unity
2. Petrine Ministry
3. Old Catholic-Orthodox Agreed Statements
4. Pastoral Applications of Canon 844.3

MEETING #20

April 20-21, 1994 — Central Diocesan Chancery
(Scranton, Pa.)
Hosted by the Polish National Catholic Church

PNCC	RCC
Rt. Rev. Anthony M. Rysz	Most Rev. James C. Timlin
Rt. Rev. Thaddeus S. Peplowski	Most Rev. Edward Grosz
Rt. Rev. Joseph Tomczyk	Most Rev. Alfred Abramowicz
Very Rev. Stanley Skrzypek	Most Rev. Alfred Markiewicz
Very Rev. Sigmund Peplowski	Rev. John Hotchkin
Rev. A. Waine Kargul	Rev. Joseph F. Mytych

Topics of Discussion
1. Pastoral Applications for Canon 844.3
2. The Ministry of Peter
3. Old Catholic-Roman Catholic Relations
4. International Bishops' Conference

MEETING #21

May 17–18, 1995 — Diocesan Chancery (Scranton, Pa.)
Hosted by the Roman Catholic Diocese of Scranton

PNCC	RCC
Rt. Rev. Anthony M. Rysz	Most Rev. James C. Timlin
Rt. Rev. Thaddeus S. Peplowski	Most Rev. Edward Grosz
Very Rev. Stanley Skrzypek	Rev. John Hotchkin
Very Rev. Marcell W. Pytlarz	Rev. Joseph F. Mytych
Very Rev. Sigmund Peplowski	Rev. Joseph Bambera
Rev. A. Waine Kargul	

Topics of Discussion
1. The Ministry of Peter within the Magisterium
2. Canon 844.3 Guidelines
3. The Ordination of Women

MEETING #22

May 22–23, 1996 — Holy Mother of the Rosary Cathedral
(Lancaster, N.Y.)
Hosted by the Polish National Catholic Church

PNCC	RCC
Rt. Rev. Anthony M. Rysz	Most Rev. James C. Timlin
Rt. Rev. Thaddeus S. Peplowski	Most Rev. Edward Grosz
Very Rev. Stanley Skrzypek	Rev. John Hotchkin
Very Rev. Marcell W. Pytlarz	Rev. Joseph F. Mytych
Very Rev. Sigmund Peplowski	Rev. Ronald Roberson
Rev. A. Waine Kargul	

Topics of Discussion
1. *Ut Unum Sint*
2. Petrine Ministry
3. PAPA article in *Our Sunday Visitor*
4. Lily, Pa.
5. Ordination of Women

MEETING #23

October 23-24, 1996 — Washington Retreat House
(Washington, D.C.)
Hosted by the Roman Catholic Church

PNCC	RCC
Rt. Rev. Anthony M. Rysz	Most Rev. James C. Timlin
Rt. Rev. Thaddeus S. Peplowski	Most Rev. Alfred Abramowicz
Very Rev. Stanley Skrzypek	Rev. John Hotchkin
Very Rev. Marcell W. Pytlarz	Rev. Joseph F. Mytych
Very Rev. Sigmund Peplowski	Rev. Ronald Roberson
Rev. A. Waine Kargul	

Topics of Discussion
1. The Canonical Status of Latin Rite Catholics Who Join the PNCC
2. Models for Unity
3. Development of the Married Priesthood in the PNCC
4. Union of Utrecht
5. PNCC Centennial Celebrations

MEETING #24

May 6–7, 1997 — Holy Cross Parish (West Patterson, N.J.)
Hosted by the Polish National Catholic Church

PNCC	RCC
Rt. Rev. Anthony M. Rysz	Most Rev. James C. Timlin
Rt. Rev. Thaddeus S. Peplowski	Most Rev. Edward Grosz
Very Rev. Stanley Skrzypek	Rev. Msgr. Thomas Green
Very Rev. Marcell W. Pytlarz	Rev. Msgr. John Strynkowski
Very Rev. Sigmund Peplowski	Rev. Ronald Roberson
Rev. A. Waine Kargul	Rev. Joseph F. Mytych

Topics of Discussion
1. PNCC Centennial Celebration
2. *Ut Unum Sint*
3. Papal Infallibility
4. The Ecumenical Directory

MEETING #25

October 28–29, 1997 — Diocesan Chancery (Scranton, Pa.)
Hosted by the Roman Catholic Diocese of Scranton

PNCC	RCC
Most Rev. John F. Swantek	Most Rev. James C. Timlin
Rt. Rev. Anthony M. Rysz	Most Rev. Edward U. Kmiec
Rt. Rev. Thaddeus S. Peplowski	Rev. Msgr. Thomas Green
Rt. Rev. Robert M. Nemkovich	Rev. Ronald Roberson
Very Rev. Stanley Skrzypek	Rev. Joseph F. Mytych
Very Rev. Marcell W. Pytlarz	
Very Rev. Sigmund Peplowski	
Rev. A. Waine Kargul	

Topics of Discussion
1. "Proposals regarding recognition by the RCC of a status of the PNCC parallel to that of the Orthodox"
2. Full Ecclesial Communion
3. Primacy of Peter

MEETING #26

April 20–21, 1998 — PNCC National Church Center (Scranton, Pa.)
Hosted by the Polish National Catholic Church

PNCC	RCC
Most Rev. John F. Swantek	Most Rev. James C. Timlin
Rt. Rev. Anthony M. Rysz	Most Rev. Edward U. Kmiec
Rt. Rev. Thaddeus S. Peplowski	Most Rev. John M. Dougherty
Rt. Rev. Robert M. Nemkovich	Rev. Msgr. Thomas Green
Very Rev. Stanley Skrzypek	Rev. Msgr. John Strynkowski
Very Rev. Marcell W. Pytlarz	Rev. Ronald Roberson
Very Rev. Sigmund Peplowski	Rev. Joseph F. Mytych
	Rev. Philip Altavilla

Topics of Discussion
1. Vatican and Eastern Catholic Churches
2. Union of Utrecht
3. Ecclesial Equivalence and Reciprocity

MEETING #27

November 4-5, 1998 — Diocesan Chancery (Scranton, Pa.)
Hosted by the Roman Catholic Diocese of Scranton

PNCC	RCC
Most Rev. John F. Swantek	Most Rev. James C. Timlin
Rt. Rev. Anthony M. Rysz	Most Rev. Edward U. Kmiec
Rt. Rev. Thaddeus S. Peplowski	Most Rev. Edward Grosz
Rt. Rev. Robert M. Nemkovich	Most Rev. John M. Dougherty
Very Rev. Stanley Skrzypek	Rev. Msgr. Thomas Green
Very Rev. Marcell W. Pytlarz	Rev. Ronald Roberson
	Rev. Joseph F. Mytych

Topics of Discussion
1. PNCC Twentieth General Synod
2. Unity with Autonomy and Identity
3. Meaning of Full Communion
4. Petrine Ministry

MEETING #28

April 14-15, 1999 — PNCC National Church Center
(Scranton, Pa.)
Hosted by the Polish National Catholic Church

PNCC	RCC
Most Rev. John F. Swantek	Most Rev. James C. Timlin
Rt. Rev. Thaddeus S. Peplowski	Most Rev. Edward U. Kmiec
Rt. Rev. Robert M. Nemkovich	Most Rev. Edward Grosz
Very Rev. Stanley Skrzypek	Most Rev. John M. Dougherty

Very Rev. Marcell W. Pytlarz

Rev. Msgr. John Strynkowski
Rev. Msgr. Thomas Green
Rev. Ronald Roberson
Rev. Joseph F. Mytych

Topics of Discussion

1. Models of Governance in the Code of Canons of the Eastern Churches
2. Reciprocity
3. Ecclesial Traditions
4. Petrine Ministry

MEETING #29

May 10-11, 2000 — Diocesan Chancery (Scranton, Pa.)
Hosted by the Roman Catholic Diocese of Scranton

PNCC	RCC
Most Rev. John F. Swantek	Most Rev. James C. Timlin
Rt. Rev. Robert M. Nemkovich	Most Rev. John M. Dougherty
Very Rev. Marcell W. Pytlarz	Most Rev. Thomas G. Wenski
Very Rev. John Z. Kraus	Rev. Msgr. Thomas Green
	Rev. Ronald Roberson
	Rev. Philip Altavilla

Topics of Discussion

1. Petrine Ministry
2. Sacramental Sharing Guidelines
3. Bonn Agreement on the Reception of Clergy
4. Memory and Reconciliation
5. New Publication of the Dialogue: *Journeying Together in Christ: The Journey Continues*

MEETING #30

October 24–25, 2000 — PNCC National Church Center
(Scranton, Pa.)
Hosted by the Polish National Catholic Church

PNCC	RCC
Most Rev. John F. Swantek	Most Rev. James C. Timlin
Rt. Rev. Robert M. Nemkovich	Most Rev. Edward U. Kmiec
Very Rev. Marcell W. Pytlarz	Most Rev. John M. Dougherty
Very Rev. John Z. Kraus	Rev. Msgr. Thomas Green
Very Rev. Paul Sobiechowski	Rev. Msgr. John Strynkowski
Rev. Anthony A. Mikovsky	Rev. Ronald Roberson

Topics of Discussion
1. Sacramental Sharing Guidelines
2. Primacy and Conciliarity in the Roman Catholic Church
3. Re-ordination of Father Jerzy Sieczynski
4. *Dominus Iesus*

MEETING #31

May 16–17, 2001 — Diocesan Chancery (Scranton, Pa.)
Hosted by the Roman Catholic Diocese of Scranton

PNCC	RCC
Most Rev. John F. Swantek	Most Rev. James C. Timlin
Rt. Rev. Robert M. Nemkovich	Most Rev. John M. Dougherty
Very Rev. Marcell W. Pytlarz	Most Rev. Thomas G. Wenski
Very Rev. John Z. Kraus	Rev. Msgr. Thomas Green
Very Rev. Paul Sobiechowski	Rev. Msgr. John Strynkowski
Rev. Anthony A. Mikovsky	Rev. Ronald Roberson

Topics of Discussion
1. Pastoral Guidelines for Sacramental Sharing
2. Re-ordination of Father Jerzy Sieczynski
3. Sister Churches
4. *Novo Millennio Ineunte*
5. Union of Utrecht
6. PNC-RC Relations at the Local Level

MEETING #32

October 24-25, 2001 — PNCC National Church Center
(Scranton, Pa.)
Hosted by the Polish National Catholic Church

PNCC	RCC
Most Rev. John F. Swantek	Most Rev. James C. Timlin
Rt. Rev. Robert M. Nemkovich	Most Rev. Edward U. Kmiec
Very Rev. Marcell W. Pytlarz	Most Rev. John M. Dougherty
Very Rev. John Z. Kraus	Most Rev. Thomas G. Wenski
Very Rev. Paul Sobiechowski	Rev. Msgr. Thomas Green
Rev. Anthony A. Mikovsky	Rev. Msgr. John Strynkowski
Rev. Robert M. Nemkovich Jr.	Rev. Ronald Roberson

Topics of Discussion
1. Reciprocity
2. PNC National Clergy Conference
3. Debate Over the Role of the Universal and Local Church Between Cardinals Walter Kasper and Joseph Ratzinger in *America* Magazine
4. Papal and Curial Pronouncements and Their Authority
5. The Role of the Papacy

MEETING #33

*May 15-16, 2002 — Vanderbilt Plaza Hotel (Nashville, Tenn.)
Hosted by the Roman Catholic Diocese of Nashville*

PNCC	RCC
Most Rev. John F. Swantek	Most Rev. James C. Timlin
Rt. Rev. Robert M. Nemkovich	Most Rev. Edward U. Kmiec
Very Rev. Marcell W. Pytlarz	Most Rev. Thomas G. Wenski
Very Rev. John Z. Kraus	Rev. Msgr. Thomas Green
Very Rev. Paul Sobiechowski	Rev. Msgr. John Strynkowski
Rev. Anthony A. Mikovsky	Rev. Ronald Roberson
Rev. Robert M. Nemkovich Jr.	

Topics of Discussion

1. *Liturgiam Authenticam*
2. Debate Over the Role of the Universal and Local Church Between Cardinals Walter Kasper and Joseph Ratzinger in *America* Magazine
3. Cardinal Walter Kasper's Prolusio from the Plenary Meeting of the Pontifical Council for Promoting Christian Unity
4. Establishment of Apostolic Administration for the Union of St. John Mary Vianney Campos in Brazil
5. Pedophilia Concerns

MEETING #34

*October 23–24, 2002 — PNCC National Church Center
(Scranton, Pa.)*
Hosted by the Polish National Catholic Church

PNCC	RCC
Most Rev. John F. Swantek	Most Rev. James C. Timlin
Rt. Rev. Robert M. Nemkovich	Most Rev. Edward U. Kmiec
Very Rev. Marcell W. Pytlarz	Most Rev. John M. Dougherty
Very Rev. John Z. Kraus	Rev. Msgr. Thomas Green
Very Rev. Paul Sobiechowski	Rev. Ronald Roberson
Rev. Anthony A. Mikovsky	
Rev. Robert M. Nemkovich Jr.	

Topics of Discussion

1. New Publication of the Dialogue: *Journeying Together in Christ: The Journey Continues*
2. PNCC Twenty-first General Synod
3. *Charter for the Protection of Children and Young People* and *Essential Norms for Diocesan/Eparchial Policies Dealing with Allegations of Sexual Abuse of Minors by Priests or Deacons*
4. Union of Utrecht
5. Constitution and Laws of the PNCC

COMPILED BY REV. ROBERT M. NEMKOVICH, JR.
Representative of the PNCC-RC Dialogue

Appendix III

Topics of Discussion Index:
Polish National Catholic-Roman Catholic Dialogue, 1989-2002

1. **Authority Given by Jesus to Peter and the Apostles:** June 1992
2. **Bishop of Rome as the Successor of Peter:** October 1992
3. **Bonn Agreement on the Reception of Clergy:** May 2000
4. **Brief History of the PNCC and Its Origins:** June 1989
5. **Buffalo Covenant:** June 1992
6. **Canon 844.3:** October 1990, May 1991, June 1992, October 1992, April 1993, October 1993, May 1994, May 1995
7. **Canonical Status of Latin Rite Catholics Who Join the PNCC:** October 1996
8. **Cassidy Visit:** November 1991
9. **Charter for the Protection of Children and Young People:** October 2002
10. **Collegiality in PNCC:** June 1992
11. **Collegiality of PNCC Bishops with the Bishops of the Old Catholic Union of Utrecht:** November 1989
12. **Collegiality of RC Bishops with the Pope:** November 1989, November 1991
13. ***Dominus Iesus***: October 2000
14. **Ecclesial Equivalence and Reciprocity:** April 1998, April 1999, October 2001
15. **Ecclesial Traditions:** April 1999
16. **Ecumenical Directory:** May 1997

17. **Establishment of Apostolic Administration for the Union of St. John Mary Vianney Campos in Brazil**: May 2002

18. **Excommunication of Bishop Hodur**: June 1989, November 1989, May 1990, October 1990

19. **Full Ecclesial Communion**: October 1997, November 1998

20. **International Bishops' Conference**: November 1991, April 1994

21. *Journeying Together in Christ*: November 1989, May 1990

22. *Journeying Together in Christ: The Journey Continues*: May 2002, October 2002

23. **Jurisdiction of Bishops of the PNCC**: May 1991

24. **Kasper's Prolusio from the Plenary Meeting of the Pontifical Council for Promoting Christian Unity**: May 2002

25. **Lay and Clerical Feelings Regarding Full Communion**: October 1992

26. **Lily, Pa.**: May 1996

27. *Liturgiam Authenticam*: May 2002

28. **Married Priesthood in the PNCC**: October 1996

29. **Memory and Reconciliation**: May 2000

30. **Models for Unity**: April 1993, October 1993, October 1996

31. **Models of Governance in CCEC**: April 1999

32. *Novo Millennio Ineunte*: May 2001

33. **Old Catholic-Orthodox Agreed Statements**: October 1993

34. **Old Catholic-RC Relations**: May 1990, October 1990, April 1994

35. **Ordination of Women**: May 1995, May 1996

36. **PAPA Article in Our Sunday Visitor**: May 1996

37. **Papacy and the Council**: November 1991, October 2000

38. **Papacy in Light of the Church as Communion**: April 1993

39. **Papal and Curial Pronouncements**: October 2001

40. **Papal Infallibility**: May 1997

41. **Pastoral Guidelines:** June 1992
42. **Pedophilia Concerns:** May 2002
43. **Petrine Ministry:** October 1993, April 1994, May 1995, May 1996, November 1998, April 1999, May 2000
44. **PNC National Clergy Conference:** October 2001
45. **PNCC Twentieth General Synod:** November 1998
46. **PNCC Twenty-first General Synod:** October 2002
47. **PNCC Centennial Celebrations:** October 1996, May 1997
48. **PNCC Constitution:** May 1991, October 2002
49. **PNCC Statutes Comparable to Orthodox:** October 1997
50. **PNCC: Its Roman Catholic Origins:** June 1989
51. **PNCC-RC Relations at the Local Level:** May 2001
52. **Primacy in the Church:** October 1990, May 1991, October 1997, October 2001
53. **Responsible Parenthood:** May 1991
54. **Sacramental Sharing:** May 1990, May 2000, October 2000, May 2001
55. **Service of Healing:** June 1992
56. **Sieczynski Re-ordination:** October 2000, May 2001
57. **Sister Churches:** May 2001
58. **Union of Utrecht:** May 1990, October 1992, October 1996, April 1998, May 2001, October 2002
59. **Unity with Autonomy and Identity:** November 1998
60. **Universal and Local Church:** October 2001, May 2002
61. *Ut Unum Sint*: May 1996, May 1997
62. **Vatican and Eastern Catholic Churches:** April 1998

COMPILED BY REV. ROBERT M. NEMKOVICH, JR.
Representative of the PNCC-RC Dialogue

Index

COMPILED BY JAMES B. EARLEY
Chancellor
Diocese of Scranton

NOTES

NOTES

NOTES

NOTES

NOTES